C#

2 books in 1:

*The New Beginner's & Intermediate
Step by Step Guide
to Learn C# in One Week.*

*Including Projects And Exercise To
Mastering C#.*

Andrew Sutherland

Table of Contents

C# for Beginners user

C# for Intermediate User

C#

New step by Step Guide to Learn C #

in One Week.

Including Projects And Exercise To Mastering C#.

Beginners User

Andrew Sutherland

Introduction

Congratulations on purchasing C#, and thank you for doing so.

The following chapters will discuss all of the different parts that we need to work with when it comes to learning how to code C#. There are a lot of options when it comes to learning how to work with some of the coding and the programming that you want to do. But one of the best options that we can choose from is the C#, and this guidebook is going to spend some time looking at what we are able to do with the C# language, and how we are able to make it work for all of our coding needs as well.

The beginning of this guidebook is going to take some time to look at how we are able to work with the C# language and some of the steps that we can bring in when it is time to make this program be on our computers and to ensure that it is going to work in the proper manner. While C# is a language that is found on the Windows system, it is possible to go through and add it to the Linux and the Mac systems as well, allowing us to have a bit more freedom with some of the codings that we want to do as well. We will discuss this and so much more as we go through this guidebook.

Once we have the program ready to go on our computer, it is time to move on to some of the actual coding that we want to do as well. We will look at how we are able to go through and install Visual Studio Community, how to write out some of our own programs in the C# language, and some of the basic parts of the code that we need to know in order to get started with coding in this language. We will even take a look at how to work on the keywords in this language and what they mean to provide commands to our codes as well.

From there, we are able to move on to some of the other things that we are able to work with when in this language. We can spend some time working with the File Input and Output of our codes, how to make some of our own conditional statements so that the program can make decisions based on the conditions that you set, and how to work with a lot of the operators that are found in this language as well.

That is just the beginning of what we are able to do with the C# language. When we have some of those basics down, it is time for us to go through and look at some of the more complex topics that need to show up when we are doing our work in C#. We will spend this time looking at what polymorphism is about, how to work with the enumeration data type, how to work with multithreading and why this is important, and how the variables work in more depth so we know why we would like to work with these.

To finish off this guidebook, we are going to spend some time looking at a few projects that you are able to bring in to ensure that you are going to get the best results out of this process. There are a lot of different parts that we tried to take a look at the inside of this guidebook, and the best way to get them all under control and to ensure that it is going to work in the manner that you would like is to get some practice. This final chapter is going to help us to get this down and will ensure that we are prepared to get started as well.

There are a lot of things that we are able to enjoy when it comes to working with the C# language. And while there may be some other coding languages that we are able to focus on as well, you will find that the C# language will be able to handle all of your coding needs in no time. When you are ready to get started with coding in the C# language, and you want to learn how to make this all work well for your coding and programming needs, make sure to check out this guidebook to help you out!

There are plenty of books on this subject on the market, thanks again for choosing this one! Every effort was made to ensure it is full of as much useful information as possible, please enjoy it!

Chapter 1: An Introduction to C#

Learning how to code is going to provide you with a ton of benefits along the way. It is going to make it easier to create some of the programs and applications that you would like. It is going to be able to help you further your career with a lot of options that are simple to work with and can allow us to get the best out of these new skills and more money as well. And then there are times when learning how to work with C# is going to be important because it will allow us to learn more about our computers and how they work.

There are a lot of great options when it is time to work with programming. Many languages have been developed to work on different projects, and sometimes they will work on different types of processes and applications as well. While many of these can be useful based on what you would like to accomplish with the language in the first place, we are going to take a look at how to work with the C# language and how great this one can be for our needs as well. Let's dive into the C# language and how to make this work for our programming needs as well.

What is the C# Language?

The first thing that we need to take a look at here is the C# language. C# is going to be an elegant and object-oriented language that is going to be helpful because it allows programmers to go through and built up a variety of robust and secure applications, all of which are going to run with the .NET

Framework. It is possible to work with C# on a variety of projects, including with Windows client applications, Web services, client-server applications, XML database applications and so much more.

When we are working with the C#, we will find that visually it is going to provide us with an advanced code editor along with some user interface designers that are more convenient to use, a debugger that is integrated, and some other tools that will ensure that it is easier to develop some of our applications based on this language.

The neat thing about the C# language is that it is not only going to be highly expressive and able to help us out with a lot of the more complicated codes that we want to handle, but it is also going to be easy to learn and simple. The curly-braces that are part of the syntax of C# is something that is going to look familiar, especially if you have worked with Java, C++, and C in the past. Developers who are good with these languages will find that it does not take that long to learn C# because of the similarities.

C# is useful because it is going to be able to simplify some of the issues that happen with the C++ language, and it is going to provide us with some powerful features including value types that can be null, delegates, enumerations, lambda expressions, and even memory access that is direct. None of these are going to be featured are available with languages like Java.

In addition to this, you will find that the C# language is going to be able to support some of the generic methods and types, which is going to help us provide increased type safety and performance, and it comes with some iterators, which enable the implementers of collection classes to help define custom iteration behaviors that will be easy to use by the client code.

Because this language is going to fit into the category of object-oriented, it is going to be able to support a lot of topics and options that fit into this category, and that we will be able to explore in more detail later on, including polymorphism inheritances, and encapsulation. All methods and variables that we use are going to be encapsulated within these definitions of classes. And it is possible for a class to inherit directly from one parent class, but it can be set up to implement any number of interfaces.

Methods in this language will be able to override accidental redefinition. When we work with C#, a struct is going to be similar to a lightweight class. This means that it is going to be a stack-allocated type that will be able to come on board and implement interfaces, but it is not going to be able to help us when supporting inheritances.

In addition to some of the basic principles that we just took a look at, you will find that C# is going to make it easier in order to develop some of the components of software through a few constructs, and these are going to include the following:

1. It is able to go through and encapsulate some of our method signatures through the use of delegates. These are going to enable some of the type-safe event notifications that we need.

2. Properties that are going to be there to work as the accessors for some private member variables.

3. Attributes, which are going to help provide declarative metadata about some of the different types when the program runs.

4. LINQ, which is going to stand for a Language Integrated Query. This is useful because it is going to provide us with some built-in query capabilities no matter which sources of data that we are going to work with.

There are a lot of benefits that we are able to see when it is time to work with the C# language and make it work for some of our needs. It is an object-oriented language that makes it easier to organize and keep things together, and when we are able to utilize the right IDE, and the .NET platform that we will talk about in a moment, we will be able to utilize it to make the powerful programs that we want, without all the complexities of the missing features that happen with other languages that are similar.

The .Net Framework

Another thing that we need to take a look at when working with the C# language is the .NET framework. This is going to be a framework that Microsoft has developed to run well on Windows. It is going to include a very big class library, which is known as the FCL or the Framework Class Library and this is going to provide us with language interoperability, which means that each language can use code that is written out in other languages, across more than one kind of language.

Programs that are written out in this kind of framework are going to be able to execute itself in the environment for the software rather than the hardware environment, known as the CLR or Common Language Runtime. The CLR is going to be an application virtual machine that will help to provide us with some different services including security, exception handling, and memory management. Because of this, the codes that are written with this Framework is going to be known as managed code. Both the CLR and the FCL that we have talked about are going to make up the .NET framework that we are talking about.

First, the FCL is going to be important. It provides us with some of the user interface, database connectivity, data access, web application development, algorithms, network communication, and more. Programmers are able to produce some software when they combine the source code they are working on with the .NET framework and some of the other libraries that are available.

This is a framework that is designed to work well with most new applications that we want to create on the Windows platform. In addition, Microsoft is going to produce an IDE that is specifically for the .NET software that is known as Visual Studio.

The .NET Framework began just as proprietary software, although it has since been standardized to help work on other options as well. Despite some of the standardization efforts that have happened, most developers expressed how uneasy they felt with some of the terms and the prospects that came with the open-sourced and free implementations. Because of that, the Microsoft company has changed the .NET development to help closely follow a contemporary model of a community-developed software project, including issuing an update to its patent that would help to address these concerns.

There are a lot of things that we are able to work with when it comes to the .NET Framework. There are methods that have been developed to work not only on the Windows systems but also with some of the other operating systems, including Linux and Mac. And it is able to help us work with a variety of languages, especially with C#, while being portable, secure, high in performance, and good with managing the memory that we need while writing out certain codes.

The C# IDE

Before we are able to get into details about how we can code, and what all we are able to do with the C# language, we need to get a better idea of what an IDE is about, and why this is such an important part of any coding that we want to do. To start, an IDE is going to be an integrated Development Environment, which is basically an application we can use to help with application development. In general, this is going to be a GUI or graphical user interface that is designed to make it easier for any developer to build software applications. Many times these are going to have more of the tools that you need.

Most of the common features, such as data structure browsing, version control, and even debugging, are going to be there to help the developer execute actions without needing to switch back and forth between the different applications that they are working with. This makes it easier to maximize the productivity because we are able to provide similar user interfaces for the components that are related, and it is going to reduce the amount of time that it takes to learn a new language. In addition, depending on the kind of IDE that you choose to go with, it can sometimes just support one language, and other times it will support many languages.

The concept that is behind the IDE is something that evolved from some simple command-based software, which at the time was not really as useful as the menu-driven software. Some of the modern IDE's are going to be used more in the context of our visual programming, while the applications in these are going to be created in a quick and efficient manner by moving the code nodes or the building blocks of programming that will generate the flowchart and structured diagrams. These can then be either compiled or interpreted based on what you hope to get out of the process.

It is important that we take the time to pick out a good IDE, and there are a number of factors that we need to consider as we work through this. For example, we need to spend time looking at the language support, operating system needs, and some of the costs. Sometimes the IDE that we want to work with will be free, but sometimes these are going to have limited features. It often depends on what you would like to design with that language, and what features are important to your coding needs.

There are a number of good IDE's out there that are available with the C# language. It is important to do some research and learn more about how these work, and which ones are going to have the features that you would like in order to get the best results. When you are able to do this, it is infinitely easier to get the codes written that you would like.

How to Work with C# On Linux and Mac Computers

While C# is considered a Windows language, it is possible for us to go through and work with it on a Linux and Mac computer as well. We may need to go through a few extra steps, and sometimes a few of the functionalities that we are used to seeing with Windows will be gone, but there are still a lot of benefits that we will see with using this option on other operating systems.

For the Linux system, the MonoDevelop IDE, which is part of the Mono Project, should be just what you need in order to develop some C# coding on a Linux computer. The easiest way for you to install this is to work with the MonoDevelop package that was developed to work with Ubuntu. Sometimes it is recommended to work with the WinForms toolkit, but this one is not going to be as efficient and easy to work with.

We can also set this language up to work on a Mac computer. The first step is to download an IDE, and Visual Studio Code is usually the best one here because it does work well with Mac and still provides you with the functionality that you need while the simplicity of use is still there. Just visit the Visual Studio website (we will go into more details about working with Visual Studio in the next chapter), and then make sure to click on the button to download to Mac. This should download what you need in a zip file.

Once you have been able to get this setup, you can unzip the file and then drag it over to the Applications folder. You should be able to download it from there. The next step is to go through and download the C# extension. You can go into Visual Studio Code and open up the Extensions that you need to make this work.

Now, as you are going through this process, you are going to notice that there is a search bar at the top of the extensions view. This is where you are going to type in "C#". The one that you need is going to be by Microsoft, so make sure to click on this one. Click to install and you are ready to go.

Remember though this process that the C# language is one that has been developed to work the best with a Windows system. So, if you are on a Windows system, you are more likely to find this language easy to use, and all of the features and functionalities that you are looking for in coding are more likely to be where you put them.

This does not mean that you are not able to get this to work on your Mac computer at all. It simply means that you need to take a few extra steps to get this setup, and it may not be as easy to accomplish some of the things that you would like. Taking some time to get familiar with the C# language on a Linux or Mac computer will be important to helping you get the best results in the process.

Chapter 2: Get Ready for C#

Now that we know a bit more about the C# language and what it is all about, it is time for us to dive in and take a look at some of the main points that come with this language and how we are able to make all of this work for our needs. In this chapter, we are going to get the environment for C# all set up and ready to go, and then we will move on to some of the ways that we can write out codes in C# and the basics to help us get the most out of the whole thing. Let's get started with the C# language and how we can use this for our needs.

How to Install Visual Studio Community

The first thing to look at here is to make sure that we have our computer ready to go. Before we can install the Visual Studio program, there are a few steps to go through, including:

1. Take a moment to check out the system requirements that are there. These are going to give us an idea of whether our computer is set up to support Visual Studio 2019. We are going to focus on this version of Visual Studio, but the steps for some of the other versions are going to be similar.
2. Apply all of the updates for Windows that are available. These are important because they will ensure that the computer is going to have all of the system components and the right security updates in order to handle Visual Studio.

3. When the updates are done, it is time to do a reboot of the system. This will help us make sure that the pending updates or installs are not going to hinder the work that we do with installing Visual Studio.

4. You may also need to go through and free up some space on your computer. Ake some time here to remove any of the applications and files that are not needed on your system. You can do this quickly and efficiently with the Disk Cleanup App.

When the computer is all set up, it is time to download the Visual Studio program. You can download this with the Visual Studio bootstrapper file. To do this one, though, you need to go to the Microsoft site for Visual Studio and click on the Download button. You can choose to install, then save before opening up the folder.

While we are at this part, we want to install the Visual Studio installer. Run the file that we talked about earlier in order to install all that we need with Visual Studio. This is a new and lightweight installer that is going to include all of the parts that we need for installing and then customizing the Visual Studio file that we need.

To start this, we need to go into the Downloads folder, double-click on the bootstrapper that is going to match or looks similar for one of the files below:

1. Vs_community.exe: This is going to be the one if you downloaded Visual Studio Community.

2. Vs_professional.exe: This is going to be the one if you are downloading Visual Studio Professionals.

3. Vs_enterprise.exe: This is going to be the one if you are downloading Visual Studio Enterprise.

If you do this, you are going to end up with a User Account Control notice. Make sure to click on yes for this one. Then you will need to go through and acknowledge that you see the License Terms and the Privacy Statement. Read through those and then click on Continue.

Then it is time for us to look at some of the steps that we need to take to choose our workloads. After the installer is set up, you can use it to help make some customizations to your installation by going through and selecting out the feature sets, or workloads, that you would like to handle. You can go through all of these now and see what they are like and what you would like to work with as well. You can always add in more features later on if you decide that you need them by going into Visual Studio and into Tools.

There are a number of optional parts that you are able to work with next if you would like, depending on how you would like to work with this. You can change the languages that this is able to support, for example. Take some time to look through these options as you go through them and decide if they are the right ones for you to use for your needs or not.

And when this is done, it is time to take the Visual Studio program and start doing some of the developing that you would like. There are a few steps that we are able to use to make this one happen, and that includes:

1. When the installation is done, you can choose the Launch button in order to get started with some of the codings and developing that you would like to do.
2. While you are on the start window, you can choose to create a new project.
3. When the search box shows up, you can enter in the type of app that you would like to create in order to see a list of templates that are available. The templates that are there will depend on which workloads you decided to go with during the installation. If you want more or different options for these templates, then you need to go through and choose different workloads.
   a. It is also possible to go through and filter out the search that you do for a specific coding language with the drop-down list for Language. Then we are able to filter these out with the Platform list or with the Project Type list as well.
4. When you have made these decisions, you will find that Visual Studio is going to open up the new project, and you are ready to go and get to work.

Writing Your First Program in C#

The next thing that we need to take a look at is how you can write out your first programs in C#. It is important to get a good look at some of the ways that you can write out a program in C# or any language that you are learning for that matter, and when we are able to actually write out a few codes, it makes things that much easier to handle along the way as well.

To help us get started with this, we need to open up our text editor, such as Notepad, and Visual Studio, so that we are ready to write out some of the codes that we need. Once you have that all opened up and ready to go, make sure to type in the code below in order to see more about how this language works:

```
class FirstProgram
{
static void Main()
{
                    Console.WriteLine("Using          C#    is
                    fun.");
                    }
                    }
```

Now you can access the command prompt and type:
                    csc FirstProgram.cs

After you issue this command, the compiler for C# will process this file and then create a .exe file in the same location as your code. For example, if you saved the original file on the desktop, you should see a new program come up called "FirstProgram.ee." right in the same place. If there is an error in the code that you wrote, you will see an error message come up.

Now you can run this application by entering "FirstProgram.exe." into the command prompt. If everything was done correctly, you should see that the command prompt will display the message: "Using C# is fun."

The Basics of Your Code

With the information above about how to write out code, it is time to go through it a bit more and learn about how each part is important to the work that we did. This will make it easier to write out some of the codes that we are looking for along the way, and this can really ensure that we can write out some of the more complicated codes at a later on. Some of the different parts of a C# code includes:

First, we need to take a look at the top line. This is going to have our identifier along with the keyword. The keyword will be any word inside the code that also has some special functions to get the compiler to work. With this keyword, just like we did in the example above, we are working to create a new class in this program. The identifier, when it is used well in this code, is going to be in charge of listing out the class, the method, and the variable. This one, in particular, is known as "FirstProgram".

Then we are going to move our way down to the third line in the code above. This is where we are going to spend time defining the method of Main()> This one acts as the starting point for any of the applications that we see on the computer. The program will be able to star tout by executing this method, regardless of the location where this is found inside of our code. There are two main words that will fit here, static and void, just like you see above. This will help us to determine which object we are going to see in the code.

Now we can skip down to the fifth line of the code. This is going to be the final part that we need to look at for now because it is going to include the message that we want to show up on the computer when the whole of this has been executed. This is going to rely on the WriteLine() method so that you can actually get it to show up in writing on the screen. It is possible to take this further and add in as many messages as you would like with the help of this part.

Along with the topics that we just went over, you may notice that there are a number of braces that show up in the code. These are important because they will divide the code up into blocks so that you can separate out the parts a bit easier. Keep in mind when you are writing out some of the codes that you want to use in C#, the semicolon is going to be important, too, just like what we see with Java and C.

Chapter 3: C# Keywords

Another topic that we need to take some time to look at is the C# keywords. These are going to be identifiers that are reserved and predefined. They are set up to have special meanings to the compiler, and will basically be the commands that the compiler is supposed to follow. You should not use these in the program as identifiers unless they will have, as a prefix, the @ symbol. For example, the @if is going to be an identifier that is valued, but it will not be since this is a keyword.

The first table that we are going to take a look at will have all of the keywords that are reserved identifiers when you work with the C# program. Then we are going to take a break from that and look at some of the contextual keywords that are available.

There is a difference between the regular keywords and the contextual keywords. For example, the contextual keywords are going to come with some special meaning but only in a limited program context, and we are able to use them ad identifiers outside of that context. This makes them a bit different than what we are able to do with some of the regular keywords as well.

In general, as we add more of these keywords to the C# in the future, we will find that they will be added into the library as the contextual keywords. The reason for doing this is to make sure that we are not breaking up or ruining some of the programs that the programmer was able to write out in earlier versions.

There are a number of keywords that we are able to utilize in order to make the C# program work in the manner that we want. Some of the most common keywords that we are able to work with will include:

While	Volatile	Void	Virtual	Using static
Using	Ushort	Unsafe	Unchecked	Ulong
Uint	Typeof	Try	True	Throw
This	Switch	Struct	String	Static
Stackalloc	Sizeof	Short	Sealed	Sbyte
Return	Ref	Readonly	Public	Protected
Private	Params	Override	Out	Operator
Object	Null	New	Namespace	Long
Lock	Is	Internal	Interface	Int
In	Implicit	If	Goto	Foreach
For	Float	Fixed	Finally	False
Extern	Explicit	Event	Enum	Else
Double	Do	Delegate	Default	Decimal
Continue	Const	Class	Checked	Char
Catch	Case	Byte	Break	Bool
Base	As	abstract		

From that point, we are able to work with what is known as the contextual keywords. These are going to be a bit different than what we are going to find with some of the other options. These are still important, but it is going to depend on the part of the code that we are working with, and what we hope to be able to get out of it all.

To start, the contextual keyword is going to be used in order to provide some of the specific meaning in the code that we want, but it will not be reserved like the other keywords that we are using here. For example, a few of the contextual keywords that we see in here, including where and partial, are going to have special meanings in two or more contexts based on how we are going to work with them. Some of the different contextual keywords that you are going to find in this kind of language will include:

Yield	Where (the query clause)	Where (generic type constraint)	When (filter condition
Var	Value	Unmanaged (generic type constraint)	Set
Select	Remove	Partial (method)	Partial (type)
Orderby	On	Nameof	Let
Join	Into	Group	Global
Get	From	Equals	Dynamic
Descending	By	Await	Async
Ascending	Alias	add	

The keywords are going to be important in some of the codings that we will do because they ensure that we are going to be able to see some of the results that we want in the process, and will make it easier for the compiler to do some of the commands that we would like as well. Make sure to learn some of these and keep them separate so that we are using them to provide the right commands, rather than getting an error in the code that we write.

Chapter 4: File Input and Output

Another topic that we need to spend some of our time working within the C# language is the idea of our files. These are going to be important because they will ensure that we are able to see some of the results that we want in our codes and that we will be able to pull out the different parts based on what we are hoping to accomplish as well.

These files are simple to work with, but there are different things that we need to do with each one to ensure that they are going to work the way that we want. We can set up the files to save some of the work that we want to do, and to organize the different parts of the code that we want to work with. It takes a bit of coding and a bit of work to make all of this come together and behave in the manner that you would like.

With some of this in mind, let's take a look at how the files are going to work in this kind of language and look at how we are able to handle the file input and the file output in the C# language.

Implementing the File Input and Output Operators

The first thing that we need to take a look at here is how to implement these operations. Programs that are able to accept some kind of input from the user are also able to process this input and then produce some kind of output. All of the languages for coding out there are going to support this in order to make it work.

The file is going to help with this as a collection of data that is stored on our disks with a specific name, as well as a directory path that needs to be followed. The file that is open for us to read and write data in is known as the stream.

To take this further, the stream is going to be a sequence of bytes that come from the source all the way to a destination through the path of communication that we set up. The two basic streams, of course, are going to be the input and output. Each of these streams will have some kind of function associated back to it. The input stream is there to help with the read operation, and then the output stream is for our write operation.

The system input and output namespace will often work with a lot of classes that are meant to help out with things that we need to get done in our code. Some of these will include reading operations, file deletion, file creation, and writing the operations as well. TO give us a better idea of how to describe some of the classes that are able to fall into this kind of namespace, we are able to look at the information below:

1. FileStream: This is going to be used to help us to read and to write from any location that we want within our file.
2. BinaryReader: This one is going to be used to help us read some of the data types that are more primitive from the binary stream.
3. BinaryWriter: This is going to be used when we would like to take those primitive data types from before and write

them into a binary format so that they can go over to a binary stream.

4. StreamReader: This is a good one to learn how to use because it is able to read the characters that we need from a byte stream.

5. StreamWriter: This is going to help us to write the characters that we would like over to a stream.

6. StringReader: This is going to be similar to the others we have talked about, but it is going to be used to help us read from a string buffer.

7. stringWriter: And again, this one is similar, but this time we are going to write into that string buffer that we are using.

8. DirectoryInfo: This one is going to be used in order to perform some operations on directions and more.

9. FileInfo: This one is important because it is going to help us to perform some operations on files.

The FileStream Class

Now that we have been able to talk about some of the different parts here, we also need to take a look at this class, in particular, a little bit. The operations for the file input and output are going to be implemented in that System IO namespace that we were talking about earlier. The user is able to work with this class in order to read, write, and close up the files.

From there, the classes that we have been able to go through and be inherited from an abstract class. This abstract class is going to be known as the Stream. A good example of the syntax that we are able to work within order to create one of the objects that will be found in this particular class of FileStream will be found below:

FileStream <objectname> = new FileStream (<file name>, <file Mode Enumerator>,

<File Access Enumerator> ,

<FileShare Enumerator>);

The FileMode Enumerator

The next thing that we need to take a look at is known as the FileMode Enumerator. This one is important because it is going to help us to define methods to open up the files that we need. It is also going to be used in order to restrict the mode where the file can be opened or the method that the file can be opened by the user. The parameters to this enumerator are going to be important because they will check out whether this particular file can be overwritten, created, or opened. The members of the enumerator that you will use here will be like the following:

1. Append: We would use this member to help us open u a file if it is already created, and then it will place the cursor at the end so that we can add some of the parts that we would like. If the file is not already there, then it is going to create a new file for us.

2. Create: This is the member that is going to help us to create a new file.

3. CreateNew: This is the member that we will use when we would like to specify which operating system that new file needs to be created in.

4. Open: This one is going to help us out by opening up a file that is already around.

5. OpenOrCreate: This member can be used because it helps to specify to the system that it should open up a file if it exists, or it should create a new file as well.

6. Truncate: This one is important because it is going to open up a new file for us. When it is opened, the file should then go through the process of being truncated, and the size of this file is then going to be at zero bytes to start.

Then we need to take a look at a few of the FileAccess Enumerators that we are able to work with. For this one, the file will be opened so that we can do operations of reading and writing on it. The enumerator here is going to be used to help us figure out whether the user would like to read the data that is found in that file, or if they would like to write data onto the file. It is possible for the user to want to do both of these operations as well. the members of this kind of enumerator that we are able to work with include ReadWrite, Write, and Read.

Then there is the FileShare Enumerator that we need to spend some time on. The enumerator here is going to contain a few constants for controlling the access that the constructors for FileStream are going to have on that particular file. The use of this enumeration here is going to be to help us define whether two applications can, at the exact same time, will be able to read the information out of the same file. Some of the members of the enumerator of FileShare will include:

1. Inheritable: This is going to allow one of our file handles to pass the inheritance over to the child processes.
2. Note: This one is going to reject the sharing of the current file that we are in.
3. Read: This one will allow the user to open up the file. The user will only be able to read the file, though, without being able to make any changes or additions or write in it at all.
4. ReadWrite: This one is going to allow the user to do whatever they would like in the file. It helps them to open up the file and either read through it, write in it, or do a combination of both.
5. Write: This is going to allow us to open up the file and write or make changes to that file.

How to Implement Reading and Writing Into Our Files

The next thing that we need to take a look at is how we are able to get the files set up so that we are able to read and write the text that is found inside of them. For this, the Stream class is going to be important. For example, this class is going to be used in order to write and read any of the data that we want in the text files. The StreamWriter and the StreamReader classes will be able to help us get this done.

The first option here that we need to take a look at is going to be the StreamReader class. This is going to be a class that has been inherited from the TextReader class, one that was kind of abstract but is still important. The class is going to be helpful here because it represents that the reader is going to be able to read through the characters that are there.

There are a few methods that we are able to work with this one in order to help work on this class. Some of these include:

1. Close: This one is going to close up the objects of the StreamReader class and stream, and then it is able to release the resources of the system that are associated with that reader.
2. Peek: This one is going to help us by returning the next character that is available, but it is not going to consume it.
3. Read: This one is going to read the character that is coming up next, or it could be a set of characters that are in the stream.
4. ReadLine: This one is going to help us by reading a line of characters out of the current system and then will help us to return that all out in a data string.
5. Seek: This one is going to allow us to be in the read and write position and will allow us to move this to any of the positions that are inside of the file.

To get a better idea of how we are able to work with this particular class and make it easy for us to read data out of any file that we would like in this language, we can work with the following code:

```
class Program
{
    public void ReadData()
    {
        FileStream    fs    =    new    FileStream("E:\\data.txt",
FileMode.Open, FileAcess.Read);
        StreamReader sr = newStreamReader ( fs );
        sr.BaseStream.Seek( 0, SeekOrigin.Begin);
        string str = sr.ReadLine();
        while ( str ! = null )
        {
            Console.WriteLine("{0}", str );
            str = sr.ReadLine();
        }
        sr.Close();
        fr.Close();
    }
    static void Main ( string[ ] args )
    {
        Program p = new Program();
        p.ReadData();
        Console.Read();
    }
}
```

Now, we are able to go through and work with this a bit more. We can see that there is a FileMode property value that we are going to use in order to open up our file, and then there is a property value of FileAccess that allows us to read the file. The file data.txt is going to be in the mode of open and will prepare the stream for the read operation. From there, we are going to see that our reader statement is there to create a new instance of this class so that the text file is able to use it.

One final thing to note here is the Seek() method. This is an important method because it is there to allow us a chance to move the read position to the beginning of our file. This is then going to allow us to read all the way through until we get to the very end of that file.

Next on the list is the StreamWriter class. This is going to be similar to the other option that we talked about, but this one is going to allow us to go further and write in the text file, rather than just reading. It is going to be an inheritance that comes from the abstract class known as TextWriter. The class is going to represent a writer, which is then able to come in and write out as many characters as they would like in that file. Some of the methods that we are going to be able to rely on when working with this class includes:

1. Close: This is going to help us to close up the object we are currently on and the stream.
2. Flush: This is going to help us clear all of the buffers for the current writer and will cause any of the data that has been buffered to be written over to the stream.
3. Write: This one is going to write what we would like to the stream.

4. WriteLine: This will help us write data specified by the overloaded parameters, followed by the end of the line.

The code below is a good one to work with because it helps us to implement this class so that it is able to accept the data from the user, and then will write all of that data into the file of our choice.

```
class Program
{
    public void WriteData()
    {
        FileStream fs = new FileStream("E://data.txt", FileMode.Append, FileAccess.Write);
        StreamWriter w = new StreamWriter(fs);
        Console.WriteLine("Enter the string")l
        string str = Console.ReadLine();
        w.Write(str);
        w.Flush();
        fs.Close();

    }
    static void Main ( string[ ] args )
    {
        Program p = new Program();
        p.WriteData();
        Console.Read();
    }
}
```

Now we are able to take a closer look at the code that we are working with here. In this code, we are going to find the FileMode property value, and this will be the Append value. Then the property value that comes with FileAccess is going to be Write in this case. We will open up the file named data.txt here and it will be in the append mode, which allows us to go through and add in more of the information that we want along with the way.

When we are in the append mode and using the code that we have above, the stream will be what we use and rely on for the write operation. When this is all said and done, we know that a new instance of the StreamWriter class is created for us to use.

Another thing that you may notice with this one is that the Flush() method is there, and it is responsible for clearing the stream buffer. At the same time, the Close() method is going to be there and can close up the stream while releasing the resources that have been associated with the stream at that time. This helps to keep it all together and working how we need it.

Being able to read and write on some of the files that you want to use in C# is going to be important. It will ensure that we are able to put together a lot of different parts, that we can view what is in one of our files, and that we are better able to even write out some new information on one of the files. Working with some of the code that we have present is going to make all of the difference when it comes to working on these files.

www.wideskills.com/csharp/file-input-and-output

Chapter 5: Making Choices and Decisions

While we are in the C# language, we need to take some time to work with the decision control statements or conditional statements. These are basically going to be the types of codes that are able to take the input from the user, compare it to the conditions that you set within the code, and then will make some important decisions on its own based on both of these.

There will be times when you write outcode, and you want to make sure that this program is able to handle some decisions on its own. You can choose to write it out so that there are specific conditions to find in the code ahead of time, and then the code is able to respond based on the input that the user has added into the computer.

The good news with this one is that there are a few options that you can choose from with these conditional statements. Each one is going to work in a slightly different manner based on what you are hoping to get out of the program as well, and how you would like it to respond to different inputs from the user. As we go through the different options, you will better be able to see how each one works and why it is such a great option for you to choose one of them along the way. Let's dive in and take a look at some of the main conditional statements available in the C# language, learn how each one is going to work, and explore some of the basics of coding with them as well.

A Look at the If Statement

The first kind of conditional statement that we want to take a look at here is known as our if statement. Out of all the conditional statements that we will look through, this one is going to be the most basic. It does miss out a bit on some of the functionality that we will see with these statements, but it does help us to learn more about conditional statements and can be useful in some situations as well, so it is important to learn.

When you handle this if statement, you will find that when it runs, the code will only provide us with a reply as long as the user gives us an input that matches with the conditions that are set in the code. When this does happen, then the code will be able to execute, and it will usually come up with some kind of message, depending on what the programmer puts into the code. Sometimes you will set it up to execute something else as well.

However, if the user comes through and puts in an input that does not match up with the conditions that we set up, then there will be nothing that shows up on the screen. This can cause some problems, which is why the if statement may not be used as much as some of the other options.

The good news out of all of this is that you will find, even as a beginner, that these if statements are easy to set up and work with. Let's take a look at the coding below to see how we can create one of these if statements in the C# language for our own needs:

If (x > 0)

```
{
    Console.Write("The value is positive.");
}
```

With the example that we listed above, there are certain things that need to happen. If the value that the user put sin is higher than zero, then the program is set up to print off "The value is positive". However, if the expression turns out to be false, or the input is less than zero, then the program will ignore the whole statement that comes after Console. Write and will move on.

A Look at the If Else Statement

As we can tell pretty quickly when we work with the if statement, there will be many situations where these statements are not going to be able to help us get things done in the manner that we want. You do not want to set up some codes that are not strong enough to handle the work that you want. It is never a good idea to set up a code where the user can put in something, and then the program just ends or freezes up. And this is where we will take a look at a new conditional statement, known as the if else statement.

The if else statement is going to be a nice one to work with because it adds in a ton of power to the code that we are doing and writing, while still allowing us to add in more than one option and handle pretty much anything that the user will add to the program. Sometimes we will only add in one or two options, but sometimes we can use the if else statement to handle a ton of options along the way as well.

To get to the point, we need to take a look at the syntax for the if else statement so we get a better understanding of how this will work in the C# language. A good example of the syntax for this one will be below:

If (the Boolean expression)

    {The statement/s you want to run if the result is true;

    }

    Else

    {The statement/s you want to run if the result is false;

    }

As you can already see with this one, there is going to be a lot more power that comes with the if else statement. This is a basic option with the if else statement, but you are able to add in some more lines to make it more powerful. With these, if else statements, if the answer is false, your code will go on to the next part of the statement to see whether or not that one is true. If there are more than two options, it will keep going down the if else statement until the answer turns out true, and then it will go and display the message that comes up.

Now that we have taken some time to talk about it, it is time to look at an example of how this will work so you can use it in your own codes:

If (x > 0)

    {

    Console.Write("This value will be positive.");

```
        }
     Else
          {
          Console.Write("The value is less than or equal to
zero.")
          }
```

You are going to find that when we work with the example above, the else clause is going to be important, or at least hidden until the Boolean expression ends up being false. It is there when the process will actually need the else statement. But if we end up getting a value that is true, then the first statement will be the one that will show up so we won't need the else statement at all.

What the Nested Conditional Statement is All About

Any time that we look through some of the new codes that come with C#, you should find that it is easier to work with two statements that we had above, or you can combine them to make a nested conditional statement for some of your codes as well. with a nested conditional statement, we are going to take one of the types of conditional statements above and place it inside of another one. The point of doing this is to add in some more complexity to the work that we want to see with coding, and can really give us a chain of conditions when they are needed.

The main thing that we have to focus on when it comes to handling any nested conditional statement is that if there is some mistake that happens when you write out the statement, it is going to cause an error in the whole thing, and it can take some time to fix. This makes them a bit difficult to handle and work with along the way so be careful.

The neat thing about them, though, and something that will make them pretty appealing is that they allow us to add in as many, or as few, levels as we would like. Even with this in mind, most professionals in this language will recommend that the nested statements stay around three levels or less so that they don't become too big of a mess along the way.

If you do end up going past the third level when working on these statements, then you may end up with something that is unruly and doesn't behave in the manner that you would like, and may not even work. As a beginner, stick with the three levels and go up to more as you get better with the coding.

Now, compared to the other two types of conditional statements, there will not be as many situations where you work with these nested statements, but they are still pretty neat to work with. If you do decide to work with a nested statement, it is important to know how they work, and some of the codings below is going to make this a possibility for you:

```
Double r = 60;
Double s = 70;
If (r ==s)
{
        System.Console.WriteLine("These numbers are equal.);
        }
```

```
Else
{
        If (r > s)
        System.Console.WriteLine("The value of the first
variable is greater than that of the second one.")'
        }
        Else
        {
                System.Console.WriteLine(The value of the
second variable is greater than that of the first one.")'
        }
}
```

With the example that we are looking at above, you will have a few options that will work with the if else clause. This will allow you to pick out the command so that the program knows what it needs to readout. This will help you to do some more with your program and will make it easier to make the program more complicated.

There are many codes that you are able to write that will rely on these conditional statements. They really help you to make the code stronger and will ensure that we are able to handle some of the inputs that our users give to us, even if we are not able to guess ahead of time what answer the user is going to add to the program. These can base the input off any conditions that we set, and will ensure that the program is going to behave in the manner that we would prefer. This makes it so much easier for us to see results and for us to make sure the program works the way that we want.

Chapter 6: Basic Math

While we are on the topic, we need to spend a bit of time taking a look at how we are able to handle some of the operators that show up in our code. These operators will ensure that we are able to put together several different parts of the code, add them, subtract them, assign values, and more. In many of the coding languages that we can learn, operators are going to show up. Even though they are an important part for us to work with, we need to remember that they are simple, and it is not something to be scared about at all.

In this chapter, we are going to spend some time looking over the basics of the C# operators so we can see what kinds are there when we would need to use each type, and more.

What is the Arithmetic Operators?

The first type of operator that we need to take a look at will be the arithmetic operators. These are pretty basic, and any of the mathematical symbols that you are used to working with, such as adding, subtracting, multiplying and so on, are going to fit into this category. It is likely that you are going to recognize most of the operators that show up in this one. So, any time that we want to work with some of these arithmetic operators remember that they are going to be in charge of helping us to tell the compiler that it is time to do some math.

With these, as long as the right mathematical symbol shows up in the code, and the numbers are put in the right position (this will depend on the answer that you want to get in the end), then the arithmetic options are going to work perfectly for your needs. With that in mind, some of the best arithmetic operators that you can work with will include:

- "+" this is the addition operator. It is going to add two operands together. So you would get x+y=25
- "-" this is the subtraction operator. It is going to allow you to subtract the value of the right-handed operand from the left-hand operand. So you would get y-x=-5.
- "*" this is the one that will tell the computer to multiply the two operands. So you could do x*y=150.
- "/" this one is the operator that will tell the computer to divide the left-hand operand with the right-hand operand. For example, y/x.
- "%" is often called the remainder of the modulo operator. It is going to divide the left-hand operand by the right operand and then returns the remainder.
- "++" is the increment operator. It is going to increase the value of the operand by one. So you would have ++x=16
- "—" programmers will often call this the decrement operator. It is going to decrease the value of the operand by one. This means that you will have —x=14.

There are a lot of times when you will need to work with these arithmetic operators, and it often will depend on whether your program will need to add or subtract or do some other kind of math along the way. It can also be helpful if you are trying to add together two parts of the code, even if they are not numbers. As you look through some of the codes that we will do in this guidebook, you are likely to see some of these show up as well.

What are the Assignment Operators?

There are times when you will use the arithmetic operators in some of the codes that you want to write. But these are not the only types of operators that you may want to work with either. Now that we know a bit about those and how they work, it is time to work with the second kind of operator in C# that we can work with, known as the assignment operators.

We are going to talk about variables a little bit more in some of the chapters that are coming up. But these are basically going to be a part of our code that is able to help us save a spot in the memory for a value of our choice. This is going to be really useful for some of the work that we want to do. But we need to make sure that we are able to assign a value to the variable. Without this, we are going to end up with an issue because we just reserved an empty spot in the memory of our computer.

The most common of all the assignment operators that we are able to choose from is pretty simple, as it is just the equal sign. This means that we can make up our variable in the code, and then just put an equal sign between this and the value that we want to assign over to the variable. The compiler will notice the equal sign and know exactly what you are trying to do.

While the equal sign is going to be the most common option, there are a few other operators that we are able to work with that fit under the umbrella term of the assignment operator. Some of these are going to include the following:

- "=" this operator will allow you to perform simple assignment operations. It is going to assign the value to a variable that you are working on at that time. For example, writing *int sample = 100* will tell the program that you want to assign 100 to the variable that is called "sample". It won't perform any extra processes on this variable or on the value involved.
- "+=" this is the additive assignment operator. It is going to add up the values of your two operands and then will assign the sum to your left-hand operand.
- "-=" programmers will often refer to this as the subtractive assignment operator. It is going to subtract the value of the operand on the right side from the one on the left side and then assign the difference to the left-hand operand.
- "*=" this operator will multiply the values of each operand and then will assign the product to the left-hand operand.
- "/=" this is when you will divide up the two variables and then take the result and assign it to the variable on the left.

When you decide that you need to add in one of the assignment operators to your code, you have to make sure that both of your operands are going to fall into the same category of the data type. In some cases, while writing codes, the operands that you choose will not end up as compatible, and using these is going to make it hard for the program to behave in the manner that you would like. So, if you do end up with an error in this one, you can go through and change this part up, checking that the data points match up to how we want, and then working from there on it as well.

What are the Relational Operators?

We have taken a look at the arithmetic operators so far. These are the ones that help us to do some of the math that we would like in our codes, and can add together numbers and parts of the code, while also working on other mathematical formulas along the way. We then went on to the assignment operators. The most common option for this is the equal sign that will help to give a value to one of the variables that you want to work with. Now it is time to move on to the relational operators and see what these are all about.

These relational operators are important to work within many codes because they make sure that we get an easy method to compare the values of two operands at the same time. Because we are able to make this comparison, these are usually going to be found inside of those conditional statements that we already talked about before.

With this in mind, we do need to take some time to look more closely at some of the types of relational operators that are available in the C# language, because there are a number of these that you can choose from. To help us make sure that this is going to work well, and that we can get a full understanding of how these work, assume for now that d = 100 and e = 150. With that in mind, some of the relational operators that are found in the C# language includes:

- "==" this is the operator that you can use to check the equality of two values. If the two values end up being equal, the operand will tell you it is true. Otherwise, the operand will tell you it is false. For example, saying the d == e would show up as false.
- "!=" this operator allows you to test the inequality of two values. If the values end up not being equal, it will tell you this is true. For example, e != d would result in a true.
- ">" this operator is used to check whether the operand on the left is greater than the operand on the right. If it is, then the operator will tell you it is true. For example, saying that e > d would be true.
- "<" this is the less than an operator, it will allow you to check whether the operand on the left side is less than the operand on the right side. If it is, you will get it to show up true, such as the formula d < e.
- ">=" this is the operand that will say it is true if the value of the operand on the left side is great then, or equal to, the operand on the right side. Otherwise, it will tell you the statement is false. For example, saying that e >=d evaluates as true.
- "<=" with this operator, you will get a true if the operand on the left side is less than or equal to the operand that is on the right side. For example, d <= e is true.

Now, with this one, we do not want to make it more difficult than it needs to be. But we have to remember that when it comes to these, we are going to end up with the result that is always Boolean. This isn't complicated. It simply means that any answer we get with these relational operators will either be false or true, and that will depend on the conditions that you add into the code.

Along with that idea, when we work with the relational operators, we have to check out whether we are working with the right amount of these equal signs. For example, if you are trying to work with the equality operator that we showed above, then there needs to be two, rather than one, equal sign. If you mix up these operators and end up with an assignment operator rather than a relational operator, the code will either not work the way that you want or there will be an error message that shows up.

What are the Logical Operators?

We have had a lot of fun taking a look at some of the different operators that we are able to handle in this language, and now it is time for us to move on to some of the logical operators that are available for our work as well. These logical operators are also going to rely on Boolean expressions as well because they are going to accept a value that is Boolean and then can provide us with a new value that is Boolean when we are all done with it. This one, just like some of the other operators out there, will accept, as well as rely on, the answers being either true or false when you are adding them to your code.

Now, when it is time to work on these logical operators that can be added into codes in C#, you will find that there are going to be four main ones that we can spend our time concentrating on. We are going to look at some of the examples of how these work below. But remember here that we are going to assume that c is true, d is true, and e is false. With this in mind, we can look at the following logical operators that can show up in our codes:

- "&&" this operator is called logical AND. It will only result in true if both operands are true. For example, d && c will evaluate to true.
- "||" this is the logical OR. This operator is going to give you a true if at least one of your operands is true. For example, c || e will result in true.
- "^" this operator is the Logical Exclusive OR, and it will result in a true if one of the operands is true. If both operands can be false or true, the operator will give you a false.
- "!" with this one, you will be able to reverse the value of your Boolean variable. For example, if you type in !d, you will get a false.

What are the Bitwise Operators?

Now that we have had some time to go through a few types of operators, especially ones that are pretty common in some of the other coding languages that you may work within other situations, it is time for us to take a look at a new kind of operator, one that may not be as common and you may not use it as often, but it is going to be important to helping you to get things done in your code. And these are going to be known as the Bitwise operators.

The Bitwise operator is going to be fairly similar to what is found with the logical operator, and in the beginning, it may seem like you are working with the exact same thing with them. The main difference between this bitwise operator and the logical operator is that the former is going to take a binary value and then will turn it into a Boolean value.

To make it simple, binary values are going to consist of 0 and 1, and will not look like the words that we are used to seeing out of the computer. Let's take a look at some of the different types of bitwise operators that we are able to work with here.

For this, let's assume that I = 0, h = 1, j =0 and g = 1

- "&" this is the operator that is known as the Bitwise AND. It is going to assign 1 to the positions where both of the operands have 1. For example, g & h will give you 1.
- "|" this is the bitwise OR. It is going to assign 1 to the positions when there is at least one of the operands with a 1. For instance, doing h | 1 will give you a result of 1.
- "^" this is the exclusive OR that will work well for binary data. Just like working with the logical values, this kind of operator is only going to give you 1 in the areas that the operand has a 1. For example, if you do g^j, you will get a result of 1.

You will find that the bitwise operator is going to take on a bit more work to accomplish compared to the other operators that we are talking about. And it is true that you will probably not spend a ton of time looking at and working on this operator in your beginner codes. But it is still an important operator to learn more about, and it is worth our time to learn how to make this work as well.

As we can see, there are a lot of different types of operators that we are able to work with, and each one will be able to help us get more things done in the long-term with some of our codes. The goal of each one is different, so it is often going to depend on what we would like to see happen in the code, and how we want it to play out for us. Make sure to take a look at some of these different types of operators and learn how you are able to use each one in some of the codes that you would like to write out.

Chapter 7: A Look at Polymorphism

The next thing that we need to focus on when it comes to working on the C# language is the idea of polymorphism. This is going to be seen in many cases as the third pillar when it comes to working with object-oriented programming, along with inheritances and encapsulation. This is an important topic that shows up in some of the more advanced parts that we will focus on with our coding, so it is important that we take a look at them now.

To start, polymorphism is going to be based on the Greek word for "many-shaped". There are two main aspects that make this a distinct thing that we need to focus on, and these will include:

1. When we get to run time, the objects that are in our derived class are going to be treated as the objects for our base classes in places, including the arrays, collections, and the method parameters. When this does happen, the objects declared type is not going to be identical to the type it was at run time.

2. The base classes that we see are going to define and implement some of the virtual methods, and then it is possible for the derived classes to override them. This means that they are able to go through and provide their own implementations and definitions as we go through this. When we get to the run time, when the client code calls up the method that we are working with, the CLR is going to look up the type of the object at run time. This is then going to be the part that will override our virtual

method. This means that in the source code, you are able to call up a method on a base class, and this is going to cause a derived class's version of the method to be executed.

The virtual methods are there to enable us to work with some groups of objects that are related but in a uniform method. For example, maybe you are doing a kind of drawing application that will allow your user to come in and create a wide variety of shapes on that drawing surface. When you start, you will not know at compile time what shapes the user will want to create because it is always hard to guess on human behavior.

However, even with this kind of challenge, this program will need to pay attention and hold onto information about the shapes we can work with, and the ones that the user creates, and then it has to be able to update them in the proper manner in response to what the user does with the mouse. The neat idea here is that we are able to work with a polymorphism in order to solve this problem with the help of two basic steps. Those steps are going to include:

1. The first step that we are able to do is create our own class hierarchy, where all of the shape classes are going to derive from some of the common base class.
2. Another option that we can work with is to bring up the virtual method, which is going to make sure that the correct method of the classes that we derive when we work with just one call back with the base class method we work with as well.

With this in mind, we need to start this out by creating a base class that we are going to call Shape, and then we need to go through and create some of the derived classes that we need, such as Circle, Triangle, and Rectangle. We can give the shape class a virtual method that is known as Draw, and then we would work to override it in all of our classes that are then derived from the original so that we can actually draw out the shape that the class is supposed to represent, and that the user is looking for.

From there, we are going to work through in creating our own List<Shape> object and then add in a Circle, Rectangle, and Triangle to this. If we would like to be able to update our drawing surface inside of this application, we will want to work with the foreach loop in order to iterate through the list and to call up the method of Draw and on each of the Shape objects that are in your list.

Even though all of the objects that are on this list have been able to declare the type of Shape that they are, it is going to be time to look at the type for the run time that will be invoked. This is going to be the overridden version of the method that is found in each class that we derived in this process if we would like.

One thing that we need to remember when we are working on this kind of process is that in this language, each type is going to be polymorphic because of all of the types, even the ones that the user is able to define on their own is going to inherit back from the object. This is a little bit different than what we are going to see with some of the other options out there, so we need to keep track over that and make sure that we are using it in the right manner because it is not found in the other languages that we want to focus on.

Another thing that we need to take a look at is the virtual members that come with this process. When we are looking at one of our derived classes and how it is going to inherit from a base class, it is going to gain all of the fields, methods, events, and properties of the base class. The one who is able to design one of the new classes will be able to choose between a few actions to take in order to make the class behave in the manner that they would like. Some of these options are going to include the following:

1. They can override some of the virtual members that are found in the base class.
2. They can go through and inherit some of the methods of our base classes without needing to override that base class at all.
3. They are able to go through and define some of the new implementations that are not considered virtual, and those are the members that are going to help us hide the implementations of our base class at some point.

We must remember though this that the derived class is able to come in and override the base class member in some situations, but only if the member of the base class has been declared as either abstract or virtual. The derived member needs to work with the keyword of override to help it indicate that the particular method we are on is supposed to participate in the invocation that we spend time on here.

In addition, the fields are not things that we are not able to turn into virtual objects. Only properties, indexes, events, and methods can turn into something virtual. When a derived class is able to go through and override a member that is virtual, that member is going to be called up, even when we get into a situation with an instance that has the class accessed as the instance of the base class we are using.

Virtual methods, as well as the properties that come with them, will enable the derived classes to go through and can make it easier to extend out the base class, without having to actually do some of the implementing that is usually needed on this method. An interface is also a good method to work with when we would like to define the method we are working with or when we would like to work with a set of methods that has the implementation left to the derived classes as well.

Another thing that we may want to work with when it comes to the idea of polymorphism is how to hide some of the base class members in with some of the new members that we want to work with. If you would like to handle some of the derived members and get them to come in with the exact name that we see with the base class member, but we won't work with some of the virtual invocations, you can work with the keyword of "new". This is a keyword that we are going to put ahead of the class member that will be the return type that we are trying to replace with this one.

The following code is going to show us how this is meant to happen:

```
public class BaseClass
{
    public void DoWork() { WorkField++; }
    public int WorkField;
    public int WorkProperty
    {
        get { return 0; }
    }
}

public class DerivedClass : BaseClass
{
    public new void DoWork() { WorkField++; }
    public new int WorkField;
    public new int WorkProperty
    {
        get { return 0; }
    }
}
```

When you have a base class member that is hidden, it is possible to still access this from the client code with the help of us being able to cast the instances of the class that is derived over to the base class instance if we would like.

Next on the list to focus on a bit is learning how to prevent the derived classes from going through and overriding the virtual members. These virtual members are going to remain virtual for an indefinite amount of time, no matter how many classes you go through and declare what is there between our virtual members and the class that was supposed to declare it in the first place.

With this one, if we want to bring out the original class, or Class A, and we have this class be the one that will declare our virtual member, and then we will have class B come in and take that member from class A. It is possible to go down the line and have class C take from the class before it, which is class B, then it is possible to inherit that virtual member as well, and it is going to do the process of overriding, regardless of whether class B went through and did the declaration that would do the override in the first place. They are going to have a bit of independence from one another along the way as well. A good example of how this is going to work will be below:

```
public class A
{
    public virtual void DoWork() { }
}
public class B : A
{
    public override void DoWork() { }
}
```

And finally, the last thing that we are going to take a look at is how we are able to access the whatever the base class for these members are from our derived classes. Then this derived part is going to be the one that is able to replace or override the property or the method, and it still has the power to access the property for that base class in the first place. But it has to be able to work with the keyword of the base. The code that we are able to use to make this action happen for our needs includes:

```
public class Base
{
    public virtual void DoWork() {/*...*/ }
}
public class Derived : Base
{
    public override void DoWork()
    {
      //Perform Derived's work here
      //...
      // Call DoWork on base class
      base.DoWork();
    }
}
```

One last thing that we need to focus on when it comes to this topic is that it is often recommended that we spend some time working with some of the virtual members and that we work with the base keyword to help us call up all of the implementations of our base class when it is time to have that member come in with their own implementation. Allowing the behavior of the base class show up is going to enable that derived class to concentrate on implementing some of the necessary behavior that is specific to the class that you just created. But if the implementation of that base class doesn't happen at all, and we never call it up, then it is going to be the sole responsibility of the class that was derived to double-check that the behavior it is using will be compatible with the behavior that we see in the base class.

Chapter 8: Enumerations

In the C# language, we are also able to work with parts that are known as enumerations. This is going to be one of the main data types that we can work with if we need it, but they are a little bit more specialized than what we see with the other options. For example, the enum type, or the enumeration type, is going to be one of the types of values that have been defined by a set of named constants of our underlying integral numeric type. To make it easier for us to define the enumeration that we are working with, we simply need to bring out the keyword of enum and then specify the names that we want to provide to the members of this type. A good example of the code that we can do that fits into this, and will help us to define the enumerator will include:

```
enum Season
{
    Spring,
    Summer,
    Autumn,
    Winter
}
```

We should know here that by default, the constant values that are going to be associated with these members are going to fall into the integer type. This means that they are going to be some kind of number and will start with zero before increasing by one following the text order definition that we want to handle in this part.

In addition, we are able to explicitly go through and specify any of the other types that are integral numerals as well if it is going to work as the underlying type for this class. We are also able to go through this and specify out the constant values that are associated, such as what we are going to see with the code below:

```
enum ErrorCode : ushort
{
    None = 0,
    Unknown = 1,
    ConnectionLost = 100,
    OutlierReading = 200
}
```

You are not able to go through and define a method inside the definition of the enumeration type, so try not to fall into the trap of doing this. To add some of the functionality that you would like to this type, we would need to create what is known as an extension method. The good news is that this is actually easier to work with than it may seem.

The default value that we are going to get with the enumeration type E is going to be the value that we will get when we work on the expression of (E) 0, even if you have zero sitting there and it is not going to correspond back to the member of our enum type at all.

It is also possible for us to go through and work with an enumeration type to help represent a choice from a set of mutually exclusive values, or we can do this same thing with a combination of choices as well. to make it easier for us to go through and do the process of a combination of choices if that is what is needed, then we need to work on a slightly different approach of having the enumeration type turn into bit flags instead.

Enumeration then is going to be a data type value in this language that is used for the most part to help us assign the string values or the names to some of our integral constraints. This is done to ensure that the program we are working on is easy to read and maintain over time.

For example, the four suits that we see on a deck of cards could be the four enumerators that we want to work with, and we know they are named Club, Diamond, Heart, and Spade, but they will then belong back to the enumerated type that we are able to list out as suit.

Another example of this would be some of the more natural enumerated types, such as directions, colors, days of the week, and even the planets. The main objective with these, no matter what the point of them is all about, is to help us to go through and provide a good definition for our own types of data. Enumeration is simple to declare because we just need to use the keyword of enum and make sure that it is found right inside of the structure, class, or namespace as well.

How We Can Turn Enumeration Types Into Bit Flags

We just took a look at how to work with some of the enumeration types and even discussed that there are times when we would want to turn this type into a bit flag. Now we need to take a look at how we are able to accomplish this kind of process too.

If you would like to work with an enumeration type in order to help us represent combination of choices, we need to define the enum members for those choices such that the individual choice that we are working with is going to turn into a bit field as well. This means that the associated values for those members need to be to the power of two. Then it is possible for us to work with the logical operators that are bitwise, such as the | or & operators so that we are able to combine the choices or intersect combinations of choices based on which one we are using.

Now, if we want to go through this and indicate that one of the enumeration types we have in our code is going to be declared as a bitfield, then we need to make sure that the right flags are applied to it. A good example of this is going to be below. And you will notice that with the example below, you are able to go through and include some typical combinations when it comes to the definition of our enumeration type as well.

[Flags]
public enum Days
{
    None   = 0b_0000_0000, // 0

```csharp
    Monday    = 0b_0000_0001, // 1
    Tuesday   = 0b_0000_0010, // 2
    Wednesday = 0b_0000_0100, // 4
    Thursday  = 0b_0000_1000, // 8
    Friday    = 0b_0001_0000, // 16
    Saturday  = 0b_0010_0000, // 32
    Sunday    = 0b_0100_0000, // 64
    Weekend   = Saturday | Sunday
}

public class FlagsEnumExample
{
    public static void Main()
    {
        Days meetingDays = Days.Monday | Days.Wednesday |
Days.Friday;
        Console.WriteLine(meetingDays);
        // Output:
        // Monday, Wednesday, Friday

        Days workingFromHomeDays = Days.Thursday |
Days.Friday;
        Console.WriteLine($"Join a meeting by phone on
{meetingDays & workingFromHomeDays}");
        // Output:
        // Join a meeting by phone on Friday

        bool isMeetingOnTuesday = (meetingDays & Days.Tuesday)
== Days.Tuesday;
```

```
Console.WriteLine($"Is there a meeting on Tuesday:
{isMeetingOnTuesday}");
// Output:
// Is there a meeting on Tuesday: False

var a = (Days)37;
Console.WriteLine(a);
// Output:
// Monday, Wednesday, Saturday
    }
}
```

This is just the beginning of what we are going to see when we work with these enumerations, and it is important to explore some more about the flags and how they can work with this process as well. if you want to work on this, it is a good idea to take the ideas a bit further and see how they are going to work for your needs as well.

System.Enum Type

Another thing that we are able to take a look at is the System. Enum type. This is an important part of the process and will ensure that we are able to add in a bit more functionality to some of the codes that we are writing out in the C# language. To start, the System.Enum type is going to be the abstract base class that is there for all of the types of enumeration that we handle. It is going to provide us with a lot of methods that we can utilize along the way in order to gain more information about the enumeration, what type it is, and what values are found inside of it.

Beginning with the 7.3 version of the C# language, you are able to start using the System.Enum in a base class constraint. This is often going to be referred back to as the enum constraint. This is going to be useful when you would like to specify that a type parameter is actually an enumeration type. It is not going to be used all of the time, but there are situations where this can be useful to learn more about as well.

Handling Some Conversions

We can also work with these enumerators to help us to handle some of the conversions that need to be done. For any type of enumeration that we want to add to our code, there is going to be a kind of explicit conversions between the type of enumeration that we focus on and the integral type that is going to be underneath it as well.

If you decide to go through, and then we can cast the value of enum to the type that is under it, the result is going to be the associated integral value that is found with this member as well. A good example of how we are able to work with the idea of conversions with our enumerations will be below:

```
public enum Season
{
    Spring,
    Summer,
    Autumn,
    Winter
}
```

```
public class EnumConversionExample
{
    public static void Main()
    {
        Season a = Season.Autumn;
        Console.WriteLine($"Integral value of {a} is {(int)a}");   //
output: Integral value of Autumn is 2

        var b = (Season)1;
        Console.WriteLine(b); // output: Summer

        var c = (Season)4;
        Console.WriteLine(c); // output: 4
    }
}
```

We are able to work with the Enum.IsDefined method, in order to help us figure out whether one of the enumeration types that we are focusing on is going to contain the enum member with the value that we are looking for. If it is there, this is going to help us to see what is present but will return a null answer if the associated value that we want to focus on is not present in our code.

For any of the different types of enumerators that we are working with, there are going to be several conversions. This is mainly the boxing and unboxing conversions that we can work with, and these conversions allow us to go to and from the System.Enum type, respectively.

Chapter 9: Multithreading

Multithreading is a unique topic that we are going to find in a lot of the object-oriented programming languages that are out there, including in the C# language. It is a bit more complicated, but it is always going to be good for us to learn a bit more about how it works, and what we are able to do with this overall.

To start, a thread is going to basically be the execution path of our program. Each of the threads that are there will define for us a unique flow of control. If you are working on an application that is going to involve some complicated operations or some that take up a lot of time, then you may find that it is a lot more helpful to go through and make sure that there are different execution threads or paths and that all of the threads are individually able to perform the job that they would like.

Threads are going to be a process that is pretty lightweight. One example of us using one of these threads in our programming would be when we would like to implement concurrent programming in one of our modern operating systems that are in use. When we choose to undertake this process with threads, it is going to help us to save on some of the waste that happens with the CPU cycle, and it will make sure that the application that is being used is as efficient as possible.

We did not have a lot of time to talk about threading in one of the other chapters, but often when threading is brought out, it is going to be used as multithreading because this allows for a lot more processes to happen overall. This is because the threading is only going to allow us to run one application at the time, and each application, with just the simple threading, is only able to take on one job at a time.

As we can imagine, some of the simple projects that we start with may be fine with some of the simple threading that we may find in other options. But many times we will work with an application that is going to be able to handle more than one task at a time. And when this is true of your own processes as well, it is time to divide them into some smaller threads, and this is where multithreading is going to come into play.

The Lifecycle of a Thread

The first thing that we need to take a look at here is the idea of the life cycle of a thread. This is going to be a process that is able to start when an object of the System Threading is there. This allows us to start our own threading class and will make sure that the process is able to end when the thread either has a chance to complete all of its execution or when we terminate it on our own.

There are a few different states that we are going to see when it comes to the cycle of one of the threads that we want to work with. And some of these states or stages will include:

1. The un-started state: This is going to be the situation when the instance of the thread can be created, but we are not going to call up the Start method.

2. The Read State: This is going to be the situation where the thread is all set up and ready to run through its actions, and it is simply waiting for the CPU cycle to be ready as well.

3. The Not Runnable State: This is going to be a thread that we are not able to execute the thread. There are a few reasons for this one including:

   a. The sleep method is what has been called up instead.

   b. There is a blockage in the I/O operations

   c. The wait method is the one that has been called up instead.

4. The Dead State: This is going to be the situation where the thread is going to either have to go through and complete the execution the whole way, or it is going to be aborted in the process.

A Look At the Main Thread

We can also take some time to look at what is known as the main thread. When we are working on some of the codes that we need in C#, we will find that the System.Threading.Thread class is going to be used in order to work with all of the different threads that are found in your codes. This one is going to allow us to not only create but also access the individual threads that we need when we want to work with an application that needs more than one thread. The first thread that we will have set up to execute in our process is going to be important though, and this is often known as the main thread.

When the C# program is able to start up its execution, then the main thread is going to be created in an automatic manner. The thread is going to be created with the help of our class known as Thread, and it can then be known as one of the child threads out of our main thread. You are able to access this thread with the property of CurrentThread in this class if you would like.

Properties of the Thread Class

While we are here, we need to take some time to go through some of the properties that are the most used and the most common when we are working with the Thread class that has been so important through this chapter so far. Some of these main methods and properties will include:

1. CurrentContext: This is going to help us to take a look at the thread that is executing at this time and will provide us with the current context as well.
2. CurrentCulture: This is going to help us to either get or set up, the culture that we would like to find on the thread we are currently using.
3. CurrentPrinciple: This is going to help us to either get or set up, the current principal that is found on our thread. This is important because it is going to be used often for the security of that thread.
4. CurrentThread: This one is going to list out the thread that is currently running.
5. CurrrentUICulture: This is going to be the one that we are able to use to either get or set up the current culture with the help of the Resource Manager. This can then help us to

figure out some of the resources that are culture-specific when it is time to run the program.

6. ExecutionContext: This is going to provide us with the object that we need in order to look through all of the information about the different contexts that are found in the thread that we are working with.

7. IsAlive: This one is going to provide us with a value that will indicate the status of execution on our current thread.

8. IsBackground: This one is going to help us to either get or set up a value that will help to indicate whether or not a thread is going to be one of the background threads or not.

9. IsThreadPoolThread: This is going to provide us with a value that will help us know whether or not that specific thread we are working with is going to belong to the thread pool that is being managed.

10. ManagedThreadid: This is going to provide us with a unique identifier for the managed thread that we are currently working with.

11. Name: This one will help us to get or set the name of the thread when we are ready to have that setup.

12. Priority: This is going to help us to get or even to set up the value that will help us to know what the priority is for this thread when it comes to scheduling things.

13. ThreadState: This is the final part of the properties that we are going to look at, and it is going to provide us with some of the value that we need when it is time to look at the states of our current thread.

Creating Threads

It is possible for us to go through in some of our codes and create any of the threads that we would like along the way. It is up to us how many we think the code is going to need as well. Threads are relatively easy for us to go through and created, we just need to make sure that we are able to go through and extend out the Thread class that we have been talking about. The extended Thread class is then going to work on the process of calling up the Start() method so that we can begin with this and then look towards the child thread execution.

There are a lot of benefits that we are able to work with when it comes to handling a lot of the different parts that we are able to work with. If you want to run things on the operating system of your choice if you would like to work with more than one application at a time. Without having to make them wait for one another along the way, the multithreading will ensure that we are able to do this all in one.

We need to make sure that we fully understand the process that comes with threading and multithreading, especially if we are working with the C# language. It may not seem like it is all that big of a deal when we get started, but it can definitely make a difference to how well our codes are going to behave and whether we are able to get more than one thing done at a time.

If we work on a system that does not allow for multithreading, then we are going to have a lot of downtime and waiting. If there is already a process up and running on the computer or the system, then all of the other processes have to stop and wait their turns before they can do anything at all. Once the first process is done, then we can work on the second, and then the third, and so on down the line until it is all done.

We can quickly see why this is going to be such a big pain to work with overall. It is never very efficient to work in this manner because it forces us to wait around to get one process done at a time, and can be slow and time-consuming. Multithreading is going to come into all of this and make it better. It helps us to actually handle more than one process at a time.

For example, you could run your anti-virus on a computer, allowing it to go through a scan, while also doing some searching online. You can download a new game or another program on your computer, and then, while the download is going on, you will be able to open up a Word document and do some work or search on social media. Without multithreading, you would just have to sit around and wait until the download is done. With multithreading, you are able to handle more than one task at a time.

One thing to remember is that the power on your computer is going to determine some of these as well. If your computer does not have a lot of power or memory with it, then this multithreading is not going to be as efficient as we would like. But with a strong computer, multithreading is going to work in a seamless manner to help us to get more done in the process as well.

There are a lot of times when we will work with multithreading, and it is definitely worth our time to learn more about it. When it comes to all of the uses that we have for the C# language, it makes sense that this multithreading is going to be used as well.

Chapter 10: The Variables

The next topic that we need to take a look at when we work with the C# language is the types and the variables. There are going to be two types that we are able to see in this kind of language, and they are known as the reference types and the value types. Variables that are considered a value type will be able to contain the data in a more direct manner while the reference type is going to store references to their data. The latter of these will be known as the objects that we are used to from before.

With the reference type though, we are going to find that it is possible for two of the variables to go back and reference the same object, and in the same manner, it is possible for the operations that we see in one variable to come back and affect the other variable as well. But when we are working with the value types, we will notice that the variables are each going to hold onto their own copy of the data and that it is not going to be possible for us to have an operation in one of them come in and affect one of the others. There is an exception to this where it will not work in this manner when we use the out and ref parameter variables in our codes.

So, we now need to go a bit more into what the variable is going to be all about. To start, the variable is just going to be the name that we are able to give out to the storage area that we find in our programs, in which the program is able to manipulate along the way as well. Each of the variables that we will find with this language will come with their own specific type, which is going to determine the layout and the size of the memory of the variable. This can also tell us a bit more about the values and the range of values that we will be able to store within that spot in the memory. It also tells us the operations that we are able to apply back to that variable as well.

The basic value types that are found in the C# language are going to be found below:

1. The integral types: These are going to include options like char, ulong, long, unit, short, byte, and more.
2. Floating-point types: These are going to include the double and the float types that we have seen so far.
3. Boolean types: These are going to be based on the idea of the value or the results being true or false.
4. Decimal types: These are going to be any of the values that are decimals.
5. Nullable types: These are going to include any of the data types that are considered nullable at the time.

Along with this idea, the C# language is going to allow us to have a few other defining types of values. We have looked at a few of these, including the reference types and the enumerators of our variables. And this would even count as the class that we talked about as well.

These variables are easier to work with than they may sound in the beginning. They have been designed to help us get a lot of work done in the process, and they will basically take a part of the memory of our system or our computers and then reserve it. Then we are able to go through and look through some of the different data types before assigning them to the variables that we have.

We have to make sure that there is some kind of value that is assigned back to the variable that we want to work with. This is going to be a bad thing because if we just have a variable without any value assigned to it, then we are just reserving some empty space in the memory of our computer. And the code is not going to pull anything up when we try to call this variable. It is always a good idea to work on assigning this value as soon as possible so you can make the program work in the right manner.

Remember back to some of those operators that we talked about earlier. We were able to work with the assignment operator in order to take control of some of the work that we were doing with these variables. Basically, we will work with the assignment operator, specifically the equal sign, to let the compiler know which value we would like to attach to that variable.

We are also able to add more than one value to our variable if we would like. This takes a little bit more work to get it all done, but you simply need to just continue working with the assignment operator, or the equal sign, to let the compiler know that you need to assign two or more values to the same variable if you would like.

How to Define the Variable

The next thing that we need to take a look at here is how we are able to define our variable. The syntax that we are going to see with this one will be below:

<data_type> <variable_list>;

Of course, this is going to just be a simple example of what we are going to see, but it gives us an idea of what we are able to do and how we can make this work in some of our own codes.

With the syntax that is above, we need to make sure that the type of data part is going to be one of the valid types of data that C# will support. This would include double, float, int, and char. And if you go through and define one of your own types of data, then this would fit in as well. in addition, the variable_list needs to go through and contain at least one, if not more, identifier names, and it should be separated out by commas along the way.

Initializing the Variables

Another thing that we are able to work with is initializing the variable. These variables are going to be initialized or assigned a value when we have an equal sign, and then we will follow that by a constant expression. The general form that we are going to see with this one is the following:

Variable_name = value;

Variables are unique in that they are able to be initialized in the declaration that you use. This means that we are able to take the code that we had above and actually add in the data type that we want to work with as well. It is as simple as that.

It is always a good idea for you to work with the variables in the right manner, and for you to make sure that you are able to initialize the variables in the proper manner. If you do not perform this in the right manner, it is possible that the program is going to produce some results that you are not expecting in the first place.

Now that we have had a chance to talk about this a bit, it is time for us to go through and look at some of the examples of the coding that we are able to do, and how we can make these variables work for our needs as well.

Lvalue and Rvalue Expressions

Other things that we need to take a look at while we are here are the known as the Rvalue and the Lvalue in C#. There are going to be several expressions that are going to show up in a lot of the codes that we are trying to do, and these are going to include:

1. The lvalue: This is going to be a kind of expression that will appear either at the left hand or the righthand side of the assignment that you are working with as well.
2. Rvalue: this is going to be an expression that could show up on the right of our assignment, but it is not going to take on the left side of the table at all.

The variables are able to be lvalues, and this is why they could often appear so that they are on the left side of the assignment at hand if that is where we would like to find them. On the other hand, the numeric literals are going to be seen as the rvalues in this and it is possible that they will never be assigned in this case, and they definitely are not going to show up on the left part of this at all. This is why we need to learn the differences here and where all of the parts are going to fall when we are doing some of the work that we want.

As we can see, there are a lot of things that we need to consider when it comes to working with the variables and learning what they are able to do to benefit our work as well. There are a lot of times when we are going to utilize these variables, so it is worth our time to learn about them and to practice a few codes with them, so we get the best benefits out of this as well.

Chapter 11: Encapsulation

The final chapter that we are going to take a look at before we go on with some of the different codes that we are able to write out in this language is the idea of encapsulation. This is going to be the process that we are able to use in order to enclose up one, and sometimes more, items into a logical or a physical package. Encapsulation, when we take a look at it in an object-oriented programming language like C#, is going to prevent access to some of the details of implementation that are there.

Encapsulation and abstraction are going to be features that are related to these kinds of languages. Abstraction is a bit different because it is going to allow us to make some of the information that is relevantly visible to the parts that need it, and then the process of encapsulation will enable the programmer to decide how much abstraction should be present. It will allow us to make parts of the code, either visible or hidden, based on how we would like those parts to be put away.

Encapsulation is going to be implemented when we work with access specifiers. This is something special in the codes that we are going to work with because it is responsible for helping us to define the visibility and the scope of a class member. There are a number of these access specifiers that we are going to find in the C# language, and some of these are going to include protected internal, internal, protected, private, and public.

Public Access

While we could take some time to look at all of these, we are going to take a look at the three most common types, and the ones that are going to have the most to do with a lot of the codes that you want to write out in C#. The first option that we are going to look at is known as the public access specifier.

This one, in particular, is going to help out some of the codes that we want to write because it is going to allow one of the classes that we have the ability to expose its member variables, and even some of the member functions to other parts of the code, including some of the objects and the functions that we are working with. Any public member will be easy to access from outside of the class. If this is something that you want to see happen at this part of the code, then you will want to work with the public access specifier. But if not, then we would want to work with one of the other options.

This is simple to do in some of our C# codes, but we need to take a look at some of the actual coding that we are able to do with this one to get the best results. We can see the code to work with these in C# below:

```
using System;

namespace RectangleApplication {
  class Rectangle {
    //member variables
    public double length;
```

```
    public double width;

    public double GetArea() {
      return length * width;
    }
    public void Display() {
      Console.WriteLine("Length: {0}", length);
      Console.WriteLine("Width: {0}", width);
      Console.WriteLine("Area: {0}", GetArea());
    }
}//end class Rectangle

class ExecuteRectangle {
    static void Main(string[] args) {
      Rectangle r = new Rectangle();
      r.length = 4.5;
      r.width = 3.5;
      r.Display();
      Console.ReadLine();
    }
  }
}
```

Take some time to type this into your compiler and see what kinds of answers you are able to get out of the process. When we look at this, we will notice that the length and the width that come with the variables here are going to be declared as public. This means that they are accessible from the Main() function using the Rectangle class that we named as r if we would like.

The member function of GetArea() and Display() can also help us to access some of these variables in a more direct manner, and we will be able to accomplish this without having to work with any kind of instance of the class at all. Then there are the member functions that we called the Display(), and we declared these as public as well. so it is going to be something that we are able to access from this class as well.

There is a lot that is going on with this kind of code that we just wrote out. But the whole point is that we are able to work on it to make the different functions and variables that we are able to work as public. This allows the main function there to access that part and will help certain codes to work in the manner that you would like as well.

Private Access

In addition to working with the public access that we just did, it is time for us to go through and work with the private access specifier. This is going to be the opposite of what we saw when we talked about the public option. This one is going to make it possible for the programmer to come in and hide some of the member variables and the functions as well from some of the other objects and the functions that are in the code.

Only the functions that are able to stick around in the same class would be able to have any kind of access to the private members along the way. In this specifier, you will find that even an instance of a class is not going to be able to come in and access any of the private members. A good example of this one is going to be in the code below:

```
using System;

namespace RectangleApplication {
  class Rectangle {
    //member variables
    private double length;
    private double width;

    public void Acceptdetails() {
      Console.WriteLine("Enter Length: ");
      length = Convert.ToDouble(Console.ReadLine());
      Console.WriteLine("Enter Width: ");
      width = Convert.ToDouble(Console.ReadLine());
    }
    public double GetArea() {
      return length * width;
    }
    public void Display() {
      Console.WriteLine("Length: {0}", length);
      Console.WriteLine("Width: {0}", width);
      Console.WriteLine("Area: {0}", GetArea());
    }
  }//end class Rectangle

  class ExecuteRectangle {
    static void Main(string[] args) {
```

```
        Rectangle r = new Rectangle();
        r.Acceptdetails();
        r.Display();
        Console.ReadLine();
      }
    }
}
```

You can take a bit of time here to type in the code and see what the output is going to be in all of this. In this example, we took some time to hide the different properties that are going to show up in some of your codes. In this example, the member variables of width and length are going to be seen as private. This means that the function of Main()will not be able to access these at all.

The functions that are found in the same part of the code, or the same class, are able to access the variables. But those functions, the Display() and the AcceptDetails() will be public, so the Main() function is able to call them up and use them as long as they work with the instance known as r, or the Rectangle class we are working with.

Protected Access

Another option in the specifiers that we get to work with is the protected access options. These are going to allow the new class, or the child class, the opportunity to access the variables and functions of that original class it is associated with. This is going to help in implementing some of the inheritances that we want to handle as well. This is something that is really going to be reserved for when we want to work with the idea of inheritances, but it is still a good thing to learn more about and understand that there is part of the encapsulation process that we are talking about here.

Internal Access

The final option that we can spend our time on is internal access specifier. This is going to allow a class to go through and expose some of the variables of a member and the functions to some of the other functions and objects, but only if they are in the current assembly. What this means that any member with this kind of specifier is accessible from any method or class that has been defined within the application in which we have defined the member.

A good example of the code that we are able to work with in order to see how this one is going to work will be the following:

```
using System;

namespace RectangleApplication {
  class Rectangle {
    //member variables
    internal double length;
    internal double width;

    double GetArea() {
      return length * width;
    }
    public void Display() {
```

```
        Console.WriteLine("Length: {0}", length);
        Console.WriteLine("Width: {0}", width);
        Console.WriteLine("Area: {0}", GetArea());
    }
}//end class Rectangle

class ExecuteRectangle {
    static void Main(string[] args) {
    Rectangle r = new Rectangle();
    r.length = 4.5;
    r.width = 3.5;
    r.Display();
    Console.ReadLine();
    }
}
}
```

Take some time to type this into your compiler and see what
results you are able to get. In this example, you should be able to
notice that the member function that we were able to label
GetArea() is not going to be declared with any of the access
specifiers that we saw before. If this were true, then the part that
would be considered our default for this if we do not go through
and mention what we would like it to be? In all cases, it would be
private.

This means that if you do not go through and actually put in which
of the specifiers that you would like, then the compiler is
automatically going to assume that it is private and that we should

keep it in this manner as well. if you don't mind whether or not it is private, then just keep it this way. But if you would like other parts to access it, then you need to go through and add in the specifier that you would like to work with.

And then there is one more option that fits in with this one that we need to look at as well. this is going to be the protected internal access specifier, and it is going to be the one that is going to allows the class to have a way to hide all of the functions and the variables that are going to be members here from the other classes and functions in your code, but it is still open to the child class that shows up in the same applications. This is also a method that we are going to work with when it comes to the inheritance features from before.

As we can see, there are a lot of times when we are going to work with the idea of encapsulation, and it is often helpful to make sure that we are granting the right permissions to our codes. In some cases, we want to have open and public access, and other times we would prefer to not have this and to keep different parts private and away from one another. This is exactly what the process of encapsulation will do for us.

Chapter 12: Simple Projects to Get Some Practice

We have spent a lot of our time in this guidebook taking a look at a lot of the codes that we are able to write out in C# and how we can make all of these parts come together for some of our own needs as well. one of the best ways to ensure that we are going to get really good with some of the codings that we want to do in this language, and to ensure that it is going to behave in the manner that we want is to do some practice along the way.

Each of the programs that you will want to write out will be a little bit different as well, and it is important for us to go through and check out the different aspects are going to work in any and all of the codes that we want to write as we go along here.

That is why this chapter is going to help us out one more time with some practice code that will result in a game that we are able to create on our own as well. This code is going to help us to learn more about some of the different parts that we have already collected and learned about along the way and will ensure that we are able to really make all of this come together for our needs as well.

In the code, you will notice that it is going to fit a lot of parts together, will ensure that we see some of the loops and the conditional statements, and can even show a lot of the comments, keywords, operators, and more in a more practical manner, and with putting them all together in one part of the code, compared to what we did before.

With that in mind, let's take a look at how we are able to create one of our own Hangman Games and get it to work not only with some practice in the C# language but also ensuring that we are able to get the most out of actually having a game that works with our own code:

Creating Hangman in C#

This is going to be the program that we will spend a bit of time on in this chapter. When you first look at the source code, it is going to be really long. And you may make the assumption that it is going to be too difficult for a beginner to learn how to do. But in actuality, the program is just long and not that complicated considering all of the parts that it needs to be able to do.

Think about what all goes into a simple game of Hangman. You need to have it pick out a random word for you, and then you need to make sure that it is going to know which letters are right and which ones are wrong based on the word that is up there. And there usually has to be a certain number of chances or the user to try out before the game is done, or they win. All of this has to show up in the code that we need to create below.

In the one below, we are going to set up a code that will have some blank boxes that show up at the top of the windows so that the letters that you guess right are going to show up there. The user is going to have to guess the letters and see if they can get them right. Of course, each time that the user, or you, goes in and makes a wrong guess, then the program is going to show another part of the hanged man. If you end up with 5 mistakes here, then you are going to lose. But if you guess all of the letters, you are going to win.

Now that we have the source code in place, it is time for us to go through a better explanation of how this is going to work. The event handler is first going to come through and help disable the button that is clicked, which will ensure that the user is not able to go in and click on all of that again. From there, it is going to spend time getting the tag property from the button, will convert that over to the letter of the button, and then will take the time to determine whether or not the letter is actually found in the word that we are currently working with.

We will not go over the whole code here because it can seem like a lot that we are dealing with, but a little bit of code can be worth our time to look over. Take a look at the code that we will have below, and see if you are able to recognize some of the parts that are there and how much you can remember from the other parts of our program:

/// <summary> /// Randomizes a word reading text file /// </summary> private void SelectWord() { string filePath = Path.Combine(Path.GetDirectoryName (System.Reflection.Assembly.GetExecutingAssembly().Location), "Words.txt"); using (TextReader tr = new StreamReader(filePath, Encoding.ASCII)) { Random r = new

Random(); var allWords = tr.ReadToEnd().Split(new[] { '\n', '\r'
}, StringSplitOptions.RemoveEmptyEntries); currentWord =
allWords[r.Next(0, allWords.Length - 1)]; // currentWord is
public variable } }

If the program determines that the letter is found in that chosen word, then the program is set up to loop through the labels of the letters. If the label is able to correspond back to the letter, then this is going to be the letter that shows up, in the right spot, on the blanks at the top of the page for the word. If there are any labels that are blank there, then the user has not been able to guess all of the letters yet, and the game will continue on.

However, if the user has been able to go through and guess all of the letters, then the program is going to display the message of "you won" and will disable all of the buttons that are on the keyboard for this part.

Now, it is also possible that the user is going to go through this and will guess a letter that is not actually found in the word. When this happens, the program is going to hide the skeleton image that is being displayed, will do the increments that are needed on the CurrentPictureIndex to show the next image of the skeleton, and then will help to display that image as well.

Through this, if the current image ends up being the last one, then this is a sign that the user has lost the game, and the program is going to display the message of "you lost" on the screen. With the code that we worked with above, this is going to disable all of the buttons of the keyboard, and it is going to make each of the labels display their letters so that we are able to look them over and see what the word was.

Of course, we can also go through and add in some more ports to this as well. if we would like, it is pretty easy to go through and invent a kind of scoring system for this game, and even go through and save some of the statistics that you need including the high scores how often you win and lose, and more in the settings for that program. The code above is definitely complicated enough, using a lot of the different components that come with the C# language, so it is fine if you want to just stick with this much and enjoy the game that you created.

Before we are done with this part, though, we have one more note to finish off with. We need to note that the dictionary we are basing this program on is going to provide us with the words that we need to make the game work, and it is going to also result in the use of words that are common in more than one dictionary. In this format, the words are sometimes going to end up being uncommon words, and that can make the game a bit more difficult to work with.

You have the option to go through and try to make this a little bit easier of a game to work with and choose the dictionary that you would like to work within the process. It could even be helpful to go through and work with a dictionary that is specific to a topic or an industry to make this work for your needs.

And that is all there is to this program. When you are able to combine together a lot of the topics that we have been able to work within this guidebook in order to create our very own game. And there are so many other parts that we are able to handle and create when we work with this kind of idea, and we bring out all of the topics that we worked on so far. The hangman game is a fun way to get some practice with those topics and to ensure that you are able to get it to work for your needs.

Conclusion

Thank you for making it through to the end of *C#*, let's hope it was informative and able to provide you with all of the tools you need to achieve your goals whatever they may be.

The next step is to start working with some of the different parts that are in this guidebook in order to help us to learn a bit more about the C# language and to learn how to make this one that you can use in order to handle any of the programs that you want to write in the process.

There are a lot of different options that we are able to work with when it is time to start coding, and the C# language is going to be a great one to work with in order to get the applications that you would like. It works with the Windows system and is attached automatically with this system, but we can also make it work with some of the other options that we have as well. This means that we are able to work with some of the other options like the Linux and the Mac operating systems, as well.

This guidebook has taken some time to look more at the different things that we are able to with the C# language as well. There are so many different aspects that we are able to handle when we work with this kind of language. We will take a look at how we can work with conditional statements, the loops, polymorphism, enumeration, and more. All of these can come together to help us create some of the different things that we want when it comes to creating our own codes as well.

When it comes to picking out a coding language to work with, there are always a lot of different options that we want to work with. Each of these is going to come with a lot of different options that we can enjoy, and it seems like each one is going to provide us with a lot of benefits. Some are great for helping us to work with some working on the web pages and web sites that we want to create, some are really good at helping us to handle some of the different games that we want to create, and some are good for helping us with some general-purpose coding that we would like to work with as well. it all depends on what you are hoping to get out of the process and what you hope to accomplish as well.

There are so many benefits to working with the C# language, and we spent a lot of time taking a look through this guidebook and learning how we can make this language do what we would like. When we are done, we can make some of our own codes and create the programs that we want that actually work this time around. When you are ready to start working with the C# for your needs, make sure to check out this guidebook to help you out.

Finally, if you found this book useful in any way, a review on Amazon is always appreciated!

C#

New step by Step Guide to Learn
C # in One Week.
Including Projects And Exercise
To Mastering C#.
Intermediate user

Andrew Sutherland

Introduction

Congratulations on purchasing *C#* and thank you for doing so.

There are plenty of books on this subject on the market, thanks again for choosing this one! Every effort was made to ensure it is full of as much useful information as possible, please enjoy!

Writing a program without knowing the environment in which it is to be run is like driving in a city without a city map. You only reach your destination by detours and by stopping to ask for directions.

Why C#

C# is basically not a new programming language, at least as far as the syntax is concerned. C# is more or less the syntax of the C ++ language family. The concept of C# has been developed from the ground up and fits 100% into the new.NET technology.

C ++ is a very complex language and therefore difficult to learn. C# is an easy-to-understand language. Since the language was newly developed, unlike C ++, it contains no annoying relics from previous versions.

There are over 20 programming languages for.NET technology. But why does C# take on a special role in the new technology?

C# is the primary language of.NET technology and was developed specifically for use with.NET. Many parts of the.NET framework are written in C#.

In addition, C# fully supports component-based programming. Components are building blocks that - once developed - can be used over and over again, even without knowledge of the internal working method, the components must be present. Components can be used independently of project and programming languages, which not least saves development time.

C# combines the high performance of C ++ with the simplicity of Visual Basic.

.NET Framework

In order to be able to program effectively with C#, one needs a little theoretical background knowledge, which concerns the so-called.NET Framework. That's why the.NET Framework is an integral part of this book. Before we get more involved with the.NET Framework, you should know that it is an integral part of.NET technology.

What Is Meant By The.NET Framework?

Primarily, it includes a conceptual platform that makes it possible to write programs and services. On this basis, different frameworks for different platform technologies have been provided so far.

C# and all the other programming languages that were and are developed for.NET, need the.NET Framework as a *run-time environment.* More specifically, the runtime environment of the.NET Framework consists of the Common Language Runtime, called CLR for short. As the name Common Language Runtime suggests, it is a cross-programming language runtime environment.

The task of a runtime environment is essentially to execute the code developed with the respective programming language. In the past, however, a separate runtime library (runtime library) usually had to be provided for each programming language - and in part also for each version - in order to be able to execute the corresponding programs. For example, C ++ the file *MSVCRT.DLL* and in Visual Basic 6 the file *MSVBVM60.DLL.* The concepts of the supplied runtime environments were and are still fundamentally different today. Cross-language support provides key benefits of the.NET Framework:

- Only one framework is needed.

- Different (and very different) programming languages can be used, depending on the level of knowledge and personal preference.

- There is exactly one runtime environment for all programming languages.

From these advantages, further derivations can be made:

- The cross-lingual integration

- The cross-language exception handling (Exception *Handling* refers to how a program should react when events occur that are not normally expected, such as errors.)

- Improved security (security can be controlled up to the method level)

- A simplified versioning (several versions can exist side by side)

Because the.NET Framework provides a cross-language runtime environment, it ensures interaction and optimal collaboration between components of different programming languages.

You now know that the.NET Framework is part of.NET technology and what it has to do. The.NET Framework again consists of three main components:

Common Language Runtime - the cross-language runtime environment

Class libraries (*Learn more* about classes and class libraries later)

ASP.NET - server-side applications for the World Wide Web

In this book we will deal in detail with these three components. The common language runtime and class libraries will come up again and again throughout the book, as will ASP.NET in the context of web services. The two components - Common Language Runtime and Class Libraries - of the.NET Framework are also referred to as Base Frame-work.

Chapter 1 - Create Types

Common Language Runtime - CLR

Common Language Runtime, CLR for short has the task of managing the execution of the code and additionally offers services that simplify development on and with the.NET Framework.

With the common language runtime, the developer takes a lot of work. One of the big advantages is the simplified memory management, ie the management of the main memory. As a programmer, they can concentrate more on the actual task and are less confronted with internals in terms of the organization of the main memory. In addition, the same data types exist in each programming language, which is very useful when using different programming languages, because you no longer have to think constantly about the peculiarities of the respective programming language. (A data type determines what type of data is stored, and where applicable - numeric data - its range of values and precision.)

Most or all of the memory management and many other tasks take over the common language runtime.

When *managed code* refers to code that is under the control of the runtime. He is not allowed to do certain things himself, for example, directly accessing the working memory; that is why the CLR, as an intermediary and overarching body, takes care of it. Only if you use managed code, you can benefit from certain advantages, such as: As the automatic memory management or cross-language integration.

The common language runtime has its own memory management, the so-called garbage collector (literally "garbage collection for inoperative data in memory"), GC for short.

Without the use of a garbage collector you have to take care of the memory management and release yourself, which is very time-consuming and error-prone and can even lead to system crashes. The Garbage Collector manages the memory automatically, that is, it controls all memory requirements of the system that is running your program, and removes all data from the memory that is no longer referenced, so that references no longer exist, or even easier expressed - which are no longer used.

Intermediate Language

Imagine, the whole world speaks a language and every inhabitant on this planet would understand it. The whole thing sounds very philosophical and is difficult to imagine in human communication. Translated to the.NET Framework, however, something like this has been created: an overarching, mediating language called Intermediate Language.

One of the concepts of.NET technology is to be independent of the operating system. Another advantage is the large number of available programming languages, which can be chosen according to the level of knowledge and personal preference, without any restrictions being imposed, for As for the use of written in a particular programming language component from another language.

But how are code parts that z. That were developed in C#, with code parts written in Visual Basic.NET or another programming language? At least here you have to say goodbye to conventional programming with their different runtime environments and rethink.

We know from the preceding sections that the.NET Framework has only one runtime environment and that all programming languages can be used and understood by the.NET Framework. The problem that arises here is the intermediate step between the program (in any

.NET programming language written) and the finished execution file. This intermediate step is solved in.NET with an intermediate code. This intermediate code is called Intermediate Language Code, or IL code for short.

This IL code is understood by the.NET Framework and can be translated into an executable file. Since the.NET Framework is between program and operating system, the operating system usually plays no role in the programming, since the.NET Framework acts as an intermediary between the operating system and the program.

For developers programming on the.NET platform, this means that initially no machine code is generated (for a particular processor), but IL code. IL code can be thought of as a code for a virtual processor, a processor that does not physically exist that is "thought", that exists only in the form of software. Such a processor-independent code is not something completely new; it is usually referred to as P-code or bytecode in other technologies. Unlike the IL code, P-code is usually only one generated programming language; You are thus platform-independent, but forced to use a particular programming language.

The concept of the IL code makes it clear why a program can be implemented in a wide range of programming languages. Regardless of which programming language is used, the readable source code (that is, C# statements, for example) is converted into the general, general IL code. The program that performs this transformation is called a compiler, the process of conversion is called compilation.

In addition to the IL code, the compilers also generate additional information files, the so-called metadata. These metadata include z. For example, information about types, members, and references from your program. The common language runtime requires metadata to B. to load the classes. Metadata, as shown in the figure below, is stored together with the IL code. The IL code is the product of various compilers and is required as the execution code for the JIT compiler.

JIT Compiler

The.NET Framework is also based on the general IL code. To generate z. For example, if the C# compiler uses IL code, this code can not be understood by the computer's physical processor. Each processor type has its own machine language. Ultimately, the computer can only use the machine the language of the physical processor. This code is called Native Code (or in German as "native code"), which roughly means "innate, original".

It follows that at some point in time the IL code still has to be translated into native code. Usually, a kind of interpreter is used for comparable purposes (P-code interpreter), but at the expense of the execution speed, since the same instructions are always recompiled, even if nothing has changed in the program. Alternatively, one could also convert the code with a compiler that generates native code. This would provide a higher speed, but the programmer would have to do the conversion manually after making any changes, and there would be other drawbacks that would compromise.NET's platform independence.

To combine the advantages of compiler and interpreter, therefore, a mixture of both approaches in the form of a so-called just-in-time compiler or jitter is used. The JIT compiler automatically converts the IL code into machine code. This happens only when needed, specifically when a program is called. This transformation goes so far that program modules that are not used are not translated by the JIT compiler. Only when the program modules are called by the user or other function calls in the program, the translation takes place. The advantage is that only very slightly speed is lost; Once the program module is over-compiled, it runs at the full execution speed of the native code.

At the same time,.NET remains platform-independent without limitation, so the IL code is not dependent on a specific environment.

The Execution

Use the C# compiler, *csc.exe,* to compile the existing code into the IL code. We will look more closely at the C# compiler later.

Suppose that you have developed a program that can perform various, very complex types of calculations and have realized these as separate modules and summarized them in a calculation class.

Now, when you perform a specific calculation, the JIT compiler looks for the entry point in the IL code and translates the affected computation module into native code. The remaining calculation modules are still available as IL code. If the same module is executed a second time, the JIT compiler does not have to translate the code again, it just re-executes the already translated and existing machine code. Only when further, not yet translated, modules are called, does the JIT-Com-Piler transform these modules into machine code. In this way, the execution is considerably accelerated. This acceleration is particularly noticeable in larger programs, as the call only translates the modules that are actually needed. The JIT compiler is even able to respond to changes in the hardware of the computer and to optimize the machine code for this purpose.

A Class Of Its Own

Before we start with actual programming, we should deal with the basics of object-oriented programming and here especially with the classes. C# is an object-oriented programming language. What constitutes a class in a programmatic sense will be described in more detail later. But for now an abstract case study to convey the basic idea of class and class design.

Generally speaking, a class is an abstract illustration of real problems of (programming) everyday life that provides a solution in itself and / or communicates it to its environment or fulfills tasks. For this purpose, classes have methods and properties that have to be combined with each other in order to solve the problems posed. (A method performs a concrete action - a property is more of a feature, so it returns information about what it's made of.) The meaning of methods and properties will be described in detail later.)

It is also interesting to know that you can not use a class directly in a program. Now, if you are a little confused and wondering why you encapsulate problems in classes in C#, and what makes all object-oriented programming meaningful, I can fix it. I did not feel the same way when I heard about classes and object-oriented programming for the first time.

Imagine a professor who distributes his scripts in the first lecture. Hundreds of students are waiting eagerly and eager to receive their personal script. It is clear that the professor did not write this script hundreds of times, but made copies of it. The original has only the professor, who teaches the material according to the script in his lectures and points out to the students what is important and what is not. The students work with their personal script and mark, for example, with a highlighter key text passages and write notes in their script.

This small lecture example is similar to a class. The working memory of a computer can be thought of quite remotely as the lecture hall of the professor in which the students are sitting. The moment the professor distributes his first copy of the original to a student to work with the copy, a script exists that is different from the original. This script of the student is called in the object-oriented programming instance.

You will now wonder where these differences are. In order to be able to hand over a copy of the script to the new student next year, you leave the original as it is - in contrast to the copy with which the students work and possibly mark passages and add notes.

A class is similar to the original of the script. So if you want to work with the contents of the script, you get a copy of the original; the student's seat in the lecture hall is similar to the space allocated to the copy of the class in memory.

In programming, this process is called instancing or instantiation of classes. From this process of instantiation, ie the creation of a copy of the professor's script, an object results. One can imagine an object as a "working copy", in reality an object is a concrete representation of the abstract description of the class.

Now, the idea that you are not working with classes but with objects of that class by forming an instance of the class should not be too difficult for you.

The Boolean Type

The boolean (also known as *boolean data type*) *data type* can take one of 2 values, true or false. The data type has a lot to do with a bit that can take only two values: 0 and 1. One might think that therefore for a variable of the type boolean only 1 bit in the working memory is occupied. Due to the special management of the main memory, however, a complete byte is actually reserved, ie as much memory as in the data type byte.

The boolean data type can be found in a program mostly for decisions in conditions. The boolean type works on the positive logic: the logical 1 means true - true and the logical 0 false.

Is This The Right Type?

In general, it is up to the programmer what type of data he decides. When choosing the right data type, however, you should think about the future, ie, the program should still work properly even if, for For example, the amount of data that is stored increases over time. Here it would be awkward to use data types that are no longer sufficient at some point. (You are well aware of the Y2K issue, which is largely due to the fact that too little memory was reserved for the year in the programs concerned, so the subsequent adjustments were costly.)

Nowadays, we usually have enough RAM and fast hardware, so you should choose the data type with a correspondingly larger value range in case of doubt. However, under no circumstances should generous data types be used. If z. For example, if it is absolutely certain that a loop will only be traversed 10 times, it would be an exaggeration to use an int data type for the affected variable. It is worth considering whether instead of a short type or even a byte type is sufficient. Another aspect is the performance (performance and speed) of a program. Since performance is not only dependent on the processor the program is running on, but also on the amount of memory used and available in a computer, you also have to worry about which types of data you are using. The long data type is slower than the int data type, because a larger amount of information is processed at the first time. It also implies that the long data type requires more memory than the int data type.

Implicit Conversions

Implicit conversions can be found in many situations. Mostly they are used unconsciously by the programmer, without them thinking much about it. This can sometimes lead to less beautiful side effects.

The implicit conversion happens automatically and can, for example, lead to a reduction in the precision of the floating point types up to the absolute representation without decimal places.

Type Conversion

In strict contrast to implicit conversion, explicit conversion requires specifying the data type into which the variable is to be converted. The conversion types in the C# programming language depend directly on the value ranges of the various data types. If you attempt to store the contents of a variable whose data type has a larger value range than the target variable, the compiler will issue an error message.

int iNumber = 0;

short sNumber = 0;

sNumber = iNumber;

The error message generated thereby is:

Implicit conversion of type 'int' to 'short' not possible.

Here, a type conversion of the variable iNumber must be made. The variable iZahl must go through an explicit conversion instruction method is known as *cast* are converted to the correct data type. The data type to be generated is written in parentheses before the variable.

The statement for the explicit conversion or for the type conversion runs z. As follows:

sNumber = (short) iNumber;

Error During Explicit Conversion

We know that all data types use a certain amount of memory. It thus becomes clear that the type conversion of data types of larger value ranges into smaller value ranges can lead to errors.

The int data type occupies 4 bytes in memory, while the short data type occupies 2 bytes. What happens if you want to convert a value of a variable of type int into a variable of type short and drop it? The following listing demonstrates the problem involved.

Avoiding Conversion Errors

Because conversion problems and overflows are commonplace in programming, C# gives you the ability to monitor such issues. As we have seen above, the compiler does not issue an error message if an out-of-range condition is triggered by the explicit conversion. We have to tell the compiler that a certain area needs to be overseen in our program.

Conversion errors usually only become noticeable at runtime and are not always obvious to inexperienced programmers. If you want to be on the safe side, you can put all statements that contain conversions in a checked block. Over time you will get a certain routine for conversions and use the checked block only where it is needed. The next listing shows you how to use a checked block.

Chapter 2 - Linq

It's a tradition that the first program you write when you start learning a programming language does nothing other than print the welcome text "Hello world!" To the console. It was no different for me. Much has happened in the meantime; so I allow myself that in the age of Internet and.NET this greeting a little bit change.

Just type in the code that will be printed afterwards, for example by using one of the Windows editors *WordPad* or *Notepad* (the latter is called Windows only as an *editor).* To do this, click the S TART button and then click A LLE P ROGRAMME. Under the Z UBEHÖR folder you should find the two editors.

If you can not find any of the editors there (which should not happen), under S TART / A LLE P ROGRAMME / Z OBEHÖR click on the entry USER and open the dialog box of the same name. Enter the command *notepad in it* and confirm your input with OK.

At the beginning, I do not want to confront you with the Visual C# development environment, as it makes it difficult to get to grips with the essentials. We'll talk more about the Visual C# development environment later.

For the exercises that we will be creating in this book, create a folder, best known *as* the top-level *examples* of drive *C :.* For each day in the book, a separate sub-folder with the number of the respective chapter is recommended. Use z. For example, use *Windows Explorer* to create the folders. The folder structure now looks something like this:

C: \
Examples \
Chapter01
C: \
Examples \
Chapter02

Create You The Library Project

The next step would be testing the class now. However, this requires an application that uses the class from the library because libraries themselves can not be executed directly. However, this is not tragic, because we originally planned to use the library class in an application as a base class.

Derivation In An Application

To switch to the classes of a dynamic library (DLL) in a program

To be able to access you must:

In the source code of the program, include the namespace of the library class (alternatively, you can access the class and its elements using fully qualified identifiers starting with the name space,

Set up a reference to the library.

When you work with the Visual C# Compiler, the development environment helps you set up and manage the references. If you follow the example with the *csc* compiler, just create a file called *Program.cs,* transfer the source code below, and compile the file with the option \ *r: CKummerkasten.dll,* which creates a reference to the library :

csc / r: CKummerkasten.dll Program.cs

If the DLL is not in the same directory as the EXE file to be created, you must specify the path to the DLL.

If the location of the library is not displayed as the location of the library, you probably have previously closed the bibliography library.

Before deriving from the library class, you should check that the class is working properly.

In the Main () method, instantiate the library class CKummerBox.

Before you can build and run the project, you still need to connect to the library that contains the class CKummerkasten code.

Chapter 3 - Methods

Basically, you do not need more than a suitable C# compiler to build C# programs (for example, Microsoft's *csc.exe*, which you already met yesterday), and an operating system with it installed.NET Framework. However, as programs become larger and more complex over time, when they need to contain multiple source files with different compiler settings, or to be outfitted with graphical user interfaces, programming with the pure C# compiler becomes more and more tedious. In this case, it pays to use a powerful development environment that actively supports the developer in programming. One such development environment is Microsoft Visual Studio 2008, which supports several programming languages at the same time, specifying which language is preferred during installation (eg Visual Basic, Visual C ++ or Visual C#). For individual programming languages, there are also free versions, the so-called Express Editions, which can be downloaded from the Internet. These free versions have a slightly reduced functionality compared to the full version of Visual Studio.

However, most of the code examples were chosen to be easy to set up with a simple code editor, with the individual compiler commands, including any options, often being included. Of course, these examples can all be easily created with the support of the Visual C# Express Edition. Where there are serious differences, it is explicitly pointed to the respective versions. Otherwise, there is general talk of Visual C#. The full version was mainly used for more advanced topics that are not supported by the Express version (like this one).

Today is dedicated to readers who want to work with Visual C# right from the start. The most important components of the development environment are presented. You will learn how to re-program the programs from this book with Visual C#. You'll also learn about the many smaller and larger features that make programming with Visual C# so enjoyable and comfortable.

Readers who prefer to write their code by hand and work with the pure *csc* compiler can simply skip the chapter and come back to it later if they want to migrate to Visual C# (or a comparable development environment).

Constants

In principle, a constant behaves exactly like a variable. The only difference is that you can not change a constant after its initialization. There are two types of constants in programming: literal constants (also called real, natural constants) and symbolic constants.

Literals Constants

This type of constant is represented by its value. Literary constants are inherently constant and thus easily recognizable as such, since the value can be found directly in the source text in typed form. Examples of literal constants are:

int i = **1** ;

double d = **3.14** ;

char c = **'a'** ;

string s = **"Hello.NET"** ;

In the example above, you see that in addition to variables, literal and symbolic constants also belong to a specific type. 1 is a value of type int and 3.14 of type double. But they are not just numeric values as constants but also a character or a string, which you then call string constants. So the single letter 'a' is of the type char and "Hello.NET" is of the type string.

So if a constant is managed just like a variable, how can you assign a data type to a literal constant? We already know the declaration of a variable:

long iNumber = 50;

This declaration shows which data type the variable iNumber contains, namely long. 50 lies in the value range of the data type long. For us, this means that the variable iNumber stores the value 50. The value 50 represents the type int by default, but this is not problematic due to the automatic implicit conversion, as you will see shortly.

Literal constants are assigned to standard types without the use of a specification suffix. By default, the numbers in the range of -2,147,483,648 to 2,147,483,647 are declared int, so the value 50 from the example above. Floating point values are declared as double.

Escape Sequences

Finally, a little digression to the so-called escape sequences, which are very practical in practice. Escape sequences are treated in detail in connection with the formatting of strings. Escape sequences are special characters that you use within string constants. You can use it to realize line breaks or format textual output in general. In addition, the escape sequences help with display or formatting problems in the source code. For example, suppose you want to double-quote a string constant. In the source code, this means that the string is hereby terminated, resulting in an error message:

string sName = "Hello, my name is" Strasser ""

To avoid error messages, you must use a special escape sequence. The compiler recognizes this special character and then inserts a double quotation mark:

string sName = "Hello, my name is \" Strasser \ ""

The syntax of an escape sequence looks like this: a backslash (\) followed by a

Letters describing the formatting. The below table lists some important escape early sequences on:

Escape sequence	description
n \	New line
\ t	Tab
\ b	Backspace
\ "	Double Quotes (")
\ '	Single quote (')
\\	Backslash (\)

The following listing shows how to use the escape sequence that wraps to a new line.

```
using system;

namespace Kap3

{

    class CDemo

    {
```

```
static void Main (string [] args)

{

    Console.WriteLine ("First Row \ n Second Row");

    Console.ReadLine ();

}

}

}
```

Instructions

A program is controlled by various instructions. However, statements also evaluate expressions that the program can continue to process. There are a large number of operators for this purpose - eg. B. +, - and * - available.

One statement that you see very often in a program is the assignment of the contents of two different variables into a variable, which are linked by an operator for this purpose:

a = boc;

The character o here represents the operator, which links the two variables b and c together. Insert   the   appropriate operator. Examples of operators are the addition sign (+) and the subtraction sign (-). The result of the combination of b and c is stored in the variable a.

Whitespaces

In addition to statements, expressions, operators and comments, there are additional characters in the source code. These characters are called *whitespaces*. They are used primarily for the clean, clear design of the source text. Surely you have already made extensive use of it, without being aware of it.

Whenever you indent lines by pressing the Tab key or by breaking lines with the Enter key, whitespaces are inserted. Usually, these characters are not visible on the screen, and most editors can also be configured to display whitespaces (usually with weak dots or arrows).

The whitespaces include the space and all characters that also create spaces, especially the tab and the line break.

Since the whitespaces are used primarily for formatting the source text, they are initially ignored by the compiler. Here are some examples of how to format statements using whitespaces.

a = b + c;

a = b + c;

a = b + c;

```
a = b + c;
```

All instructions do the same. In the first line, all characters were written next to each other, which does not produce a very readable code. In the two subsequent lines, the variables and operators were visually separated by whitespaces, resulting in a much clearer code. In the fourth example, the use of whitespaces has been exaggerated (extra line break), which undermines the readability of the statement.

You should make extensive use of whitespaces to indent and otherwise visually separate statements, blocks, and other elements in your code so that the code remains clear and legible.

However, whitespaces are not always ignored by the compiler. If you use spaces and tabs within a string (data type string) or Characters (char), these characters become part of the data stored in the string or character. For example, the string "Hello.NET" stores a space between the two words "Hello" and ".NET".
The following two statements have the same result, although in the second statement a newline was inserted in the method name Console.WriteLine (this method outputs text to the console). The line breaks only change the formatting of the source text. Only in the string "Hello.NET" is the space output:

```
Console.WriteLine
```

```
("Hello.NET");
```

Console.

WriteLine

("Hello.NET");

Incidentally, you can only use the space and the tab within a string or character:

Console.WriteLine ("Hello →.NET");

In the example, the two words are separated by the tabulator - here represented symbolically by an arrow (→) -, whereby in comparison to the normal space a much larger horizontal distance is achieved.

However, linefeeds may not be used within a string or character:

Console.WriteLine ("Hello.NET ");

Here, within a string, the following line was broken, resulting in the following error message.

Is expected line
feed in constant

As you can see, not all types of whitespaces are ignored. Over time, however, you will develop a sense of how and where you can and may use Whitespaces.

Empty Instructions

Over time, when you see other C# programs, you'll see a lone semicolon in a line here and there. Such instructions are called blank instructions. You can see such empty statements, for example, in for loops. Such instructions do not do anything. At this point, it should suffice to mention that they exist and that they are permissible in the programming language C#. A small example of a permissible empty instruction can be seen here:

```
for (a = 0; a <10; Console.WriteLine (a ++));
```

Composite Statement And Blocks

We have already described the need for blocks to increase the clarity in a program. Such blocks are also called compound statements and combine a set of statements in a curly bracket. A block always starts with an opening curly bracket { and ends with a closing curly bracket }. The following example shows you such a block.

```
{

WriteLine ("{");

WriteLine ("Hello");

Console.WriteLine (". NET");
```

```
WriteLine ("}");

}
```

You can see blocks in programming in different ways:

```
{Inst
ructi
on; i
nstr
uctio
n;

}

{

instruction;

instruction;

}
```

All these types of blocks are permitted and used in practice. The differences lie exclusively in the formatting of the source text, that is, as far as indents and line breaks are concerned.

I do not want to put a stop to your creativity, but get used to one of the block diagrams above and do not invent your own. These illustrated block statements will be found in most programs.

If at some point you expand or modify a third-party program, continue to use formatting as introduced by the developer of the program. There is hardly anything worse in a source code than inconsistent formatting.

Expressions

An expression can be part of an instruction. Ultimately, expressions are also to be seen as instructions. In C#, anything that returns a value and consists of one or more elements (such as numeric values or variables) is an expression. In short, anything that returns a value is an expression, and there are virtually unlimited possibilities in C#.

Thus, symbolic or literal constants and variables return expressions.

The following statement has four expressions.

a = b + c;

Of course, the three variables are also expressions, each of which contains a value of its own - before the instruction is executed - e.g. B. can evaluate with the debugger. But where does one find the fourth expression? The statement itself is an expression, since it gives the value of the addition of b and c. Do not let it irritate you; the next example will give you clarity.

If a = b + c is an instruction and at the same time an expression, since a = b + c returns a value, then the following statement should also be valid.
z = a = b + c;

True, this statement is also valid, since a = b + c is also an expression.

If b contains the integer value 5 and c the integer value 4, then it is clear that a represents the integer value 9, provided that all variables with the data type int have been declared. The expression a = b + c also contains the integer value 9. Thus, the variable z also represents the value 9.

A included in this example, the addition of the variables b and c. The value of a is always the sum of the two variables b and c, and thus also the value represented by the variable z.

Regarding the order in which expressions are evaluated, the rank order "point before line" plays a major role; which should be well known to you from school. One speaks of the ranking of the operators. So not all expressions are evaluated equally, but first the multiplication (operator *) and divisions (/) are evaluated and then the additions (+) and subtractions (-) are evaluated.

z = a * b + c;

The expression a * b returns a value here, which is then added to the value of the variable c, which makes the entire statement an expression again.

Operators

Operators make it possible to link an expression, an instruction or several expressions and instructions with each other. In the previous sections, you have already encountered various operators. The expressions or statements that are linked by an operator are called operands. The following example shows you a simple link based on an addition.

a = b + c;

The plus sign (the symbol for the addition) is here the operator; the two variables b and c (elements of the link) represent the operands. In C# there are a large number of such operators:

Assignment operator
Mathematical
Operators
Remainder
operator
Decrement and increment
operators
Composite operators
Comparison operators

Logical operators

Conditional operator

Comma operator

Assignment Operator

We have often used the assignment operator. The symbol for the assignment operator is the equal sign =. But do not confuse the assignment operator in C# with the equal sign ==, which can be found in formula collections and equates or compares two variables. For the comparison of values there is another operator in C#, which we will get to know later.

If you want to write one value of a variable into another variable in C#, you assign the variable to another. This looks like this:

a = b;

But b does not mean that the two variables are identical in value, but that the value of variable b is written in variable a. Only after carrying out this assignment do the two variables have the same value.

Mathematical Operators

We all know the basic accounting types and their operators. Which includes:

Addition

Subtraction

Multipl
ication

Divisio
n

The general notation of mathematical links looks as follows.

a = boc;

Let's write a small application with the operators + and -. The program polls two numeric values from the user via the console. After entering these, a calculation is carried out and the result is output.

Remainder Operator

The remainder operator returns the remainder of a division with integers. For example, 5 modulus 4 is 1 because dividing 5 by 4 leaves the value 1. The remainder operator is represented in C# by the character %.

There are a number of applications in which the remainder operator can be used. For example, suppose that you want to output a dataset line by line and create an interline after every 10th line to achieve better optical separation. In this case you can perform a calculation of *line number* modulus 10. If the line number is divided by 10, this division will arrive at every 10th line without remainder - you will get 0 and can get 0. Whenever 0 is returned, make an interline.

The remainder operator works only with integers and therefore does not accept floating-point numbers. This can be z. B. in the division of integers to take advantage by further processed in addition to the actual result of the division and the remainder of the division. The following program reads two integers and divides the first number by the second number. The remainder of the division is calculated using the remainder operator %.

Increment and Decrement Operators

In loops or conditional iterations, a variable is usually used as a counter variable, a so-called counter. Its task is to increase or decrease its value by 1 each time. This process of increasing is called incrementing and decrementing the opposite, namely decreasing the value by one. C# contains special operators for such operations.

There are various ways to increase the value of a variable by one or decrease it by one.

a = a + 1;

b = b - 1;

a ++;

b--;

++ a;

--b;

The first way to change the value of a variable by one, we already know. If a = a + 1, the current value of variable a is incremented by one and written back to variable a. The same procedure is used at b = b - 1, except that here the value is reduced by one.

The other four examples a ++, b--, ++ a, --a principally execute, increment and decrement the same actions. This type of representation or the type of these operators is called unary operators [4] Unary operators only affect one operand.

But what is the difference between a ++ and ++ a or b-- and - b ? If they appear as a single statement in a row, no difference is noticeable at first. Only in combination with an extended instruction results in a difference, in addition more.

Ranking And Parentheses

If you want to perform calculations in C#, you should know about the ranking of the operators. As a rule, one can fall back on the knowledge of mathematics lessons in school.

a = 5 + 4 * 2;

What about the ranking of the operators in C#? First the term 5

4 and then multiplied by a factor of 2 ?

a = 9 * 2;

Or is the rule that we know from school days - point by line - used?

a = 5 + 8;

As already indicated in the previous sections, in the basic arithmetic operations in C# the rule is point by line, the result is therefore 4 * 2 + 5 = 8 + 5 = 13. Thus, the operator * has a higher priority than the + operator. There are other operators in C#, so you can not get ahead with the rule "dot before line" alone. Here, a well-defined ranking of the operators is used, according to which calculations are performed.

The multiplicative operators come second. Do not let the word confuse you multiplicatively. Every division can also be expressed as multiplication. So is z = a / b;

equivalent to

z = a * 1 / b;

The additive operators come in the ranking at the end. The same principle applies again to the order of priority as above. You can express the pressure

z = a - b;

also as

z = a + -b;

write. Consider again the example from above.

z = a * 1 / b;

This expression contains several operators with the same priority. Here is a simple rule. If, as in this example, there are several multiplicative operators in an expression, the result is evaluated from left to right. This means that first the result of the multiplication a * 1 is calculated and then the result is divided by the value of the variable b.

The analysis of the following listing illustrates the effects of the ranking of operators.

```
using system;

namespace Kap3

{

class CDemo

{

static void Main (string [] args)

{

int a = 10;

int b = 5;

int c = 2;

int z = 0;


z = a * 1 / b;

z = a + -b;
```

```
z = b / c * a;

z = a * b% 20;



z = a ++ * b - a;

z = ++ a * b - a;



Console.ReadLine ();

}

}

}
```

Let's start with line 14. These are just multiplicative operators that have the same priority. First the result of a * 1 is calculated and then divided by the value of the variable b. The content of the variable z is thus the value 2.

In line 15 we see an additive and a unary operator. The unary operators are prioritized over the additive operators and thus calculated first. The unary sign operator reverses the sign of the contents of variable b. If there is a negative number here, the value becomes positive and vice versa. Then the value of the variable b is added to the variable a. Thus, the content of variable z is 10 + -5 = 10 - 5 = 5.

Lines 17 and 18 follow the rules described in line 14. First of line 17: The value of the variable z in this line is 20. Should it not yield 2.5? Please note, however, that an integer data type is used so that the decimal places are ignored; therefore, the result is not 2.5, but 2 (which results in 2 * 10 = 20 for z). To line 18: The result of the variable z is the value 5 * 10% 20 = 50% 20 = 10. Here you can see very well that operators of equal priority are linked from left to right.

Lines 20 and 21 are a bit more delicate. Here exist unary, multiplicative and additive operators. First to line 20:

z = a ++ * b - a;

Unary operators have the highest priority. a ++ increments the value in line 20, but only after the value has been read out. This is the postfix notation. The value of the variable a is in this case 10 (and not about 11) and is multiplied by the variable b (10 * 5 = 50). Only after this operation is a raised by one.

Now is the outcome of 50 the value of a withdrawn, a but now has the value 11 because a is incremented after read. This results in 50 - 11 = 39. Now to line 21:

z = ++ a * b - a;

Here, the variable a initially still has the value 11. Since the prefix notation is used now (++ a), the value is already incremented before reading out, so it has the value 12. This results in 12 * 5 - 12 = 60 − 12 = 48.

The calculation of expressions is controlled in C# by means of the ranking of operators. But what if you want to control your calculation yourself? Here is the possibility to put the preferred expression in parentheses. Parentheses override the order in which variables are linked, regardless of which operator is used. Let's try changing the priority in favor of addition in the following example.

```
z = a ++ * b - a;
```

If the content of variable a is 10 and b is 5, we already know from the previous listing that z is 39. If we now want to change the priority in favor of the addition, we have to put a brace around the expression b - a.

```
z = a ++ * (b - a);
```

What do you think about the result for the variable z ? Let's get back to our knowledge. C# usually evaluates expressions from left to right. The multiplicative linking of the variable b to the variable a ++ was canceled by the parenthesis and thus the entire expression b - a is linked multipliatively. In the variable a is the value 10, which is multiplied by the expression b - a. However, the expression b - a contains the variable a, which of course was previously incremented by one. So the expression follows:

z = 10 * (5 - 11);

Before the multiplication takes place, the parenthetical expression is evaluated.

z = 10 * -6;

The content of the variable z is thus the value -60.

Comparison Operators

The comparison operators have the task of comparing expressions with each other and thus of answering queries. However, every query has a serious limitation, as a result it returns only yes or no. So it is not possible to ask a question such as "In which directory is the file named *xyz.txt* ?". But you can write a routine that can answer the following question - "Is the file named *xyz.txt* in this directory?".

Such expressions can be edited using comparison operators. C# works with the positive logic. Thus, a question that is answered with yes results in true (true); a question that has no result, but false.

Do not confuse the assignment operator = with the comparison operator == !

If a value is assigned to a variable, for example, to be able to perform calculations, then use the assignment operator. Here, the content of the variable is manipulated. The content of variable a has the value 5 here :

a = 5;

If, on the other hand, one compares a variable with a value or another variable in order to be able to make decisions, for example, then the comparison operator is used. In this case, the content of the variable is not manipulated.

a == 10;

The content of the variable has the value 5 and not the value 10.

Here, the entire expression returns false.

Programs that execute only one instruction after the other would hardly be needed in practice for the typical problems to be solved - they would lack a certain (artificial) intelligence. However, to be able to make decisions about a program requires special instructions, which are summarized in the so-called sequential control.

A branch in the program flow has at least one condition and from this condition a resulting statement. The result or value of a condition can only contain two states: true or false.

The state within the sequence control results from the positive logic. If the value of the condition is true, then the statements that are in the branch block are executed. However, if the value of the condition is false or false, the statements in the branch block are ignored.

The easiest way to make a decision in a program is to use the if statement. The syntax of this branch looks like this:

if
(co
ndit
ion)

inst
ruct
ion;

or

if (condition)

{

    Instructions;

      ...;

      ...;

```
}
```

If there are several statements in a branch block, this is called a compound statement. If the condition is met, all instructions contained in the compounding guide will be executed.

The if statement does not terminate with a semicolon.
In general, if statements are used in conjunction with expressions that are compared with each other. The following listing shows the use of if statements.
Else clause

We now know the if statement, which helps us to make decisions in a program according to certain criteria. If a condition occurs, the instructions in the instruction block are processed.

The statements in an else clause are executed if the condition of the if statement is not met. The else clause is also referred to as an alternate branch. On the one hand, the else clause increases the readability of an if statement, on the other hand, one does not want to and can not consider all the condition cases in larger programs.

The syntax of an if - else statement looks like this:

```
if (condition)

    statement1;
```

```
else

    statement2;
or

if (condition)

{

    Instructions;

    ...;

    ...;

}

else

{

    Instructions;

    ...;

    ...;

}
```

The following listing shows how to use an if - else statement. The course of the program is such that with an order value of less than 100 euros, the port costs of 5 euros are added to the order value. From an order value of 100 euros the postage costs are taken over by the sender. In addition, a discount of 100th part of the order value is subtracted.

Chapter 4 - C# Style Conventions And Nesting

In principle, it is up to every programmer how to format his source code. But if you write a source code that you still want to read and understand after a few months, or work in a development team, then you should stick to some rules. The write conventions shown in previous examples in conjunction with the if statement and if - else statement, and their nesting capabilities apply to all program blocks. This includes loops such as while, do while, for etc., as well as the construction of classes and namespaces.

The structuring of the source code is an important aspect of programming.

This type of block is space-saving and still very legible. Some programmers are annoyed by the dropped curly braces (as we have used until now, which can also be seen in the following source code); They therefore choose this spelling. But you should already have some practice for this.

```
using system;

namespace NsX

{

    class Class1
```

```
    {

        static void Main (string [] args)

        {

        }

    }

}
```

In this case, the blocks containing the further instructions are issued. The disadvantage of this structure is that the number of lines increases significantly. However, the affiliation of the instructions is very clearly recognizable in this type of representation.

```
using system;

namespace NsX

    {
        class Class1

        {

            static void Main (string [] args)
```

```
        {

            }

        }

    }
```

This notation deviates from the previous one only by the indentation of the blocks. The disadvantage of this is that the line length increases. If you have a large number of hierarchically separated blocks in the source code, you often have to scroll horizontally in order to capture the complete line, which affects readability.

Should you ever have the problem that important parts of the source code are too far to the right, so you have to scroll horizontally, you can also move a block out - right to the left edge. Often then a comment with the content <- is inserted in the block, which symbolizes that the following block that has been pushed out actually belongs here in the hierarchy, accordingly the end of the release is again marked by a comment <-. The following example shows such a case.

```
namespace NsX

    {
```

```
class Class1

{

    static void Main (string [] args)

    {

        if (condition)

        {// <-

if (condition)

{

    ...

}

...

        } // <-

    }

}

}
```

Often an instruction block has only one instruction executed on one condition. In this particular case, you are free to choose whether the block is dropped off with curly braces.

```
if (condition)

{

    statement1;

}

statement2;
```

is synonymous with:

```
if (condition)

    statement1;

statement2;
```

In both cases, statement1 is executed when the condition is met. Statement2 is always executed because it does not belong to the conditional statement block.

Branches can also be nested arbitrarily.

```
if (condition 1)
```

```
    statement1;

else

    if (condition2)

        statement2;

statement3;
```

In the example above, the else clause contains another branch that executes statement 2 if condition 2 is met. Instruction3 is always executed.

Conditions are also expressions that can be combined with single expressions. Logical operators serve to execute multiple comparisons in one condition at a time.

Imagine a login system in which you can only log in on weekdays. Here, three criteria must be met. »Is today's day a business day AND does the user exist in the system AND does the password match?« In order to evaluate such expressions, we have three logical operators at our disposal.

Condition Operator

A simple if - else statement can also be implemented using the conditional operator. Use this only for simple expressions; otherwise the readability of the source code suffers. The condition operator ? : belongs to the group of ternary [5] operators. The question mark (?) Initiates the expression to be executed when the condition is met. The colon marks the beginning of the expression to be processed if the condition is not met. The if -else statement:

if (condition 1)

    statement1;

else

    statement2;

can therefore also be written as

Condition1? Expression1: expression2;

Chapter 5 - Input / output and strings

In the previous chapters we have created a basis for working with the programming language C#. Next we'll look at the input and output as well as the strings.

Here you learn:

- how to format numbers

- how to create custom styles, how to format dates and times,

- which classes and methods are used to manipulate strings, how to use escape sequences correctly.

Strings And I / O

In the C# language, all strings represent instances of the System.String class of the common language runtime. There are a variety of methods in this class that help us manipulate strings.

We already met strings. In our previous examples, it was all about string constants.

"I am a string constant"

String constants are always in double quotes. If a string constant has only alphanumeric characters, output to the console will not be a problem. The string constant will be output as it is in the source code.

Console.WriteLine ("I am a string constant");

The WriteLine () method of the Console class specifies the string

I am a string constant in the console. This output of the string constant to the console is also called "outgoing data stream".

Data streams are supported in C# bidirectionally, ie in both directions. The console can only output or receive the data type string. For the programmer, this means that he has to perform a conversion when entering (or receiving) data to his program. Would you like z. For example, to process the weight of a person in their program typed by a user in the console, the weight must first be converted to the appropriate data type. The class Convert is available for this purpose.

double dWeight = Convert.ToDouble (Console.ReadLine ());

Console.ReadLine passes the program a data stream of type string. Since the implicit conversion from the data type string to a data type double does not work, an error occurs without conversion. In principle, all data streams that are transferred from the console to the program must be converted, with the exception of the string data type itself. However, the Convert class does not protect you against incorrect entries. If you try to convert a letter to a double data type, you will receive an error message.

An unhandled exception of type System.FormatException occurred in mscorlib.dll.

This error message shows you how the data stream of the console works. For example, the letter x does not correspond to the format of a data type double. The data type thus depends on the format of the input. This does not mean, such. For example, the format mark of the decimal point / point is displayed (at 5.5 or 5.5). The decisive factor is the data type of the value to be processed. Only then can you perform arithmetic operations by entering the weight.

Formatting With Escape Sequences

Programs should not only work properly, they should also be easy to use. The input mask presented to the user should be largely self-explanatory and concise. It follows that we need to format the output to the console accordingly. This is where the escape sequences help. This is to be discussed in detail. Escape sequences allow you to output certain special characters as well as characters that have a special meaning for the C# compiler. A classic problem is the double quotes "". Just write these into a string constant

Console.WriteLine ("I am a string constant");
you get an error message from the C# compiler. The double quotes for the C# compiler mean that the text between two quotes is interpreted as a string constant, in the example, "I am a". After that, the compiler expects an expression or the end of the statement. The remainder of the string constant actually belonging to the text to be output is ignored. So the C# compiler looks at the above line in the form

Console.WriteLine ("I am one"

Of course, the closing bracket and the semicolon are missing here. This is exactly one of the error messages that the C# compiler outputs.

What to do if you want to output one or more double quotes in the output. In this case you use the corresponding escape sequence.

\ "

Escape sequences always start with a backslash, followed by a wider-res character. The escape sequence \ " prints a double quotation mark ("), which solves the previous problem easily.

Console.WriteLine ("I am a \" string constant \ "");

As output in the console you get then

I am a "string constant"

Format Numbers

The C# programming language not only provides escape sequences for formatting the output, but also special characters for formatting numbers. These formatting characters have their own syntax in C#.

Standard Formatting Of Numbers

When you format numbers, you will most often use the standard formatting provided by the C# programming language. Depending on how you want to represent numbers, there are various possibilities.

Would you like z. For example, to output an integer, that is, values of type int, with a certain number of decimal places, use the formatting character d. Use this character to specify the desired number of digits. B. d5 for 5 digits.

...

int iNumber = 200;

...

Console.WriteLine ("Number: {0: d5}", iNumber);

...

The value of iNumber is given by the formatting with two leading zeros.

Number: 00200

The number of decimal places specified by the d formatter are minimum digits. Use instead the number 200000, this is not reduced to 5 digits.

In mathematical applications or scientific results one often uses the exponential representation. Again, the programming language C# offers a convenient formatting option, the character e, which you can use to set the desired number of decimal places to be output:

Console.WriteLine ("Number: {0: e3}", iNumber);

The output of the value 200 is now in the form

2,000e + 002

2,000e + 002 means $2,000 * 10^2 = 2,000 * 100 = 200$.

Another example: The value 123456789 is output with the help of the formatting symbol e10 :

1,2345678900e + 008

Formatting Floating Point Numbers

In conjunction with floating-point numbers, C# provides two formatting characters that can be used to influence the number of decimal places: f and n. To do this, write the desired number of digits behind one of the characters. The difference between the two formatting marks lies in the representation of the thousands places. First of all, an example.

...

double dNumber = 12345.54321;

...

Console.WriteLine ("number: {0: f}", dzahl);

...

If you use the format character f without a position, the default value of two decimal places is output:

Number: 12345.54

An example of formatting values with five decimal places:

Console.WriteLine ("number: {0: f5}", dzahl);

To improve the readability of large floating-point numbers, the C# programming language provides the ability to mark thousands of digits with a separator (thousands of points). For this one uses the formatting mark n. So gives the formatting

Console.WriteLine ("number: {0: n5}", dzahl);

the number

Number: 12.345,54321

with the thousands separator and five digits after the decimal point.

If you limit floating-point numbers to a certain number of decimal places, you do not have to worry about rounding the decimal places. This is done by the formatting or the C# compiler for you; it will be rounded up or down accordingly.

Currency Format

C# makes it easy to format a number as a currency. When specifying the currency, the country-specific setting of the computer is used. The default setting of the decimal places of the currency format is 2. So there

...

double dBetrag = 199.99;

...

```
Console.WriteLine ("Amount: {0: c}", dBetrag);
```

...

the amount with two decimal places and the currency information.

Amount: 199.99 _

Again, the automatic rounding of the output works.

```
Console.WriteLine ("Amount: {0: c1}", dBetrag);
```

Amount: 200.0 _

Special Formatting

The programming language C# offers two further formatting types:

Formatting in hexadecimal
numbering system general formatting

With the help of hexadecimal numbers you can eg. For example, the contents of memory addresses can be rendered more elegantly and efficiently than would be possible with decimal values. Thus, the number 10 in the decimal number representation corresponds to the letter A or a in hexadecimal representation. For hex values, the format characters x and X are offered. First of all to x :

...

int iNumber = 10;

...

Console.WriteLine ("Hex: {0: x}", iNumber);

...

The following line appears in the output

Hex: a

So lowercase letters are output. However, if you prefer uppercase letters, use the X formatting character :

Console.WriteLine ("Hex: {0: X}", iNumber);

The output now looks like this:

Hex: A

The same case-sensitivity of the formatting characters also works with the exponential representation.

For the so-called *general formatting* the formatting marks g and G (*general)* are offered. This type of number representation is the least expensive and makes sense if there is only limited space available for the output, but the numerical information is to be reproduced unadulterated. Here the C# compiler decides which type of representation is used.

Custom Formatting

Although C# has a whole range of formatting options, not all cases are covered in practice by far. For example, no volume unit liters is offered by default. However, there is the possibility to create user-defined formats.

0 Formatting

If you need leading zeros for the output of a number, you can do so by custom 0 formatting. Custom 0 formatting also supports the representation of floating-point numbers.

...

int i = 54321;

double d = 12345.54321;

...

WriteLine ("{0: 00000000}", i);

For 0-formatting, write a 0 (the number) for each decimal place to be displayed. In the example, each value is output with 8 digits. The zeros in the formatting are overwritten by the number shown. The value 54321 (variable i of type int) is therefore represented with three leading zeros:

00054321

For floating-point numbers, you must explicitly specify the decimal places in the formatting. If you want to output the value of variable d with three descendants, the formatting will look like this

WriteLine ("{0: 00000000,000}", d);

With this type of formatting, the decimal places are automatically rounded as in the standard formatting. So we get at the issue

00012345.543

also three leading zeros and additionally three decimal places.

Cross-Formatting

In the so-called cross-formatting, the # character serves as a general placeholder without special fill characters such. For example, if we use the variables of the previous section, then the statement represents

WriteLine ("{0: #}", i);

no special formatting policy, the output is without special

Characteristics:

54321

The advantage of cross-formatting is that you can insert arbitrary characters as separators at specified positions in the number, and this approach can be combined well with leading zeros and decimal places. The formatting

WriteLine ("{0: 0 ## - ###}", i);

returns a special combination of numbers with leading zeros and the hyphen (-).

054-321

Of course, the cross-formatting can also be used to represent floating-point numbers. So gives the instruction

WriteLine ("{. 0: # 00}", d);

the value 12345.54321 of variable d with two decimal places :

12345.54

Formatting Groups

Grouping numbers is needed relatively often. We already know one kind of grouping - the thousands separator. But in practice, a variety of other groupings occur, for. For example, the ISBN number, bar code numbers, etc.

This type of representation can be easily implemented in C# in combination with the formatting characters 0 and #. The following example contains some examples of how to group numbers. But there are two exceptions that may cause errors in the general grouping, as they are reserved.

Percent Formatting

When outputting values that are to be displayed in percent format, no additional, manual multiplication by 100 is necessary. With the help of the formatting character %, a value is automatically converted to a percentage value and formatted accordingly.

Here is an example: First, the variable dMwSt of type double is assigned the value 0.16 :

...

double dMwSt = 0.16;

...

The result is output using percent formatting.

Console.WriteLine ("{0: #%}", dMwSt);

We get the issue 16%.

Literals Formatting

Let us remember that various units of measure, eg. For example, liters are not supported by C# by default. This problem can be counteracted with literal formatting, with which, for. B. the unit liter can be mapped.

Here we need in our program special formatting, which also includes the liter.

Suppose, for example, that the current capacity of a milk boiler should be expressed in one liter. For this we only need to include the word *liter* in our formatting.

...

int iFuel = 100000;

...

Console.WriteLine ("{0: #, # liter}", iFuel);

This gives us the output

100,000 liters

Case Formatting

In special cases, you have to format numbers differently, depending on whether they are negative, positive or null. Case formatting makes such dependent formatting easy and convenient. The three cases (for negative, positive and zero) are written next to each other in the formatting string and separated by semicolons (;).

Format Date And Time Values

Of course, before we start formatting dates and times, we need to know how to create dates and times in C#. For this the class DateTime is offered. From this class we use the properties for the further use of date and time values

Now

and

Today

The Now property returns the current date and time as the datetime type.

WriteLine (DateTime.Now);

deliver us

06.06.2002 17:22:03

The Today property returns the current date. Since the datetime type is used again, the dummy time 00:00:00 is returned next to the date.

WriteLine (DateTime.Today);

returns the following:

06.06.2002 00:00:00

The two properties Now and Today of the DateTime class can not only return a complete date and time value, but also individual components.

Output of Enumerations

You know that these are realized by the enum data type. When outputting enumerations, there are also formatting characters available that formulate the value less, but rather determine what is displayed - the stored value (string) itself or the numeric value to which it is assigned.

Compare Strings

You probably know the annoying input masks in which you have to enter the user name and password. What usually happens here is that strings entered by the user are compared to values stored in the program or stored in a database. For such and other purposes C# offers different methods and properties.

Insert, Delete and Replace

The programming language C# has convenient options for inserting, copying, replacing and deleting within strings. For this we have the following methods available.

Insert (Start Pos, String2) adds the string String2 from the position Startpos in the current string.

Remove (Startpos, Number) deletes the specified number of characters from the position Startpos.

Replace (search string, new string) replaces the substring search string with the string NewString. The replacement takes place globally, ie if the substring occurs several times, all occurrences are replaced.

Preparing Strings

Often, user input or data that has been read in other ways, such as A database, not the expected format. For example, in practice, leading blanks often need to be removed. For such tasks, C# provides the following methods:

Trim () removes all leading and trailing spaces in a string.

ToUpper () converts all characters of a string to uppercase.

ToLower () converts all characters of a string to lowercase.

PadLeft inserts so many spaces at the beginning of a string that the string is stretched to the length of new_string_length.

PadRight appends so many spaces to a string that the string is stretched to the length of new_string_length.

Substring (Pos start, number) returns a substring with the length number from the current string, starting from PosBin.

Chapter 6 - Flow Control

Sequential control systems are special instructions that control the execution (control) of programs. Using only instructions, the program runs strictly sequential. The various variants of scheduling, with their variety of control structures, allow the programmer to react to certain conditions or repeat instructions until a condition occurs.

Branches

In the C# programming language, there are three ways to branch within a program. They are the keywords if, else and switch. The simplest way to create a branch is the if statement. If the comparison of an expression matches a condition, the instructions are executed. There is also the possibility to control a condition and to take an alternative branch in case of non-fulfillment. For this we need the if-else statement. The switch statement allows us multiple selections where the various statements can be executed in a greater number of choices. Again, there is an alternative branch.

If statement - Review

An if statement controls a statement block and executes the code it contains only when the condition is met. The syntax of an if statement - depending on its formulation - looks like this:

```
if
(co
ndit
ion)

inst
ruct
ion;

or

if (condition)

{

    instruction;

}

or

if (condition)

{

    instruction;

    instruction;
```

...

}

The behavior of an if statement depends on the expression of the condition.

If the if statement is to execute only one statement, one can use the curly ones

Omit parentheses. But it does not hurt if you have the curly

Brackets sets, quite the contrary, the code is clearer.

The following example shows that there can be undesirable results if you do not set a statement block. Suppose you need an if statement that checks two numbers for equality. For this we use the variables i and j. These variables both have the value 5. The variable i should be output and then the value of the variable j should be decremented by 1. In the following form, however, the if statement becomes

if (i == j)

    WriteLine (i);

    J--;

do not fulfill the intended purpose. From the if statement

if (i == j)

depends only the instruction

WriteLine (i);

from. The instruction

J--;

will be executed in any case. If several statements depend on one condition of an if statement, they must be written in curly braces. The correct source code that fulfills the task looks as follows:

if (i == j)

{

WriteLine (i);

J--;

}

In daily programming everyday tasks often arise that can not be solved with an if statement alone.

The problems in everyday life are usually complex processes that can not be solved with a single if or if-else statement. If there is a possibility of selection, this can include further options. In this case, nested multiple if statements and if-else statements are nested. This nesting is called *nested conditional statements*.

Switch Statement

If you use a condition that has more than two alternatives, you could use multiple if or if-else constructs for it, but this does not lead to a very clear code. An alternative to this is the switch statement. This allows the selection of any number of alternatives in a hierarchy and thus corresponds to several if-statements in a row. The switch statement is also known as *multiple selection* or *case discrimination*. The syntax of the switch statement looks like this:

switch (expression)

{

    case constant_expression1:

    [Instructions)

    break, goto case N;]

```
case constant_expression2:

    [Instructions)

    break, goto case N;]


...


...


...

case constant_expression...:

    [Instructions)

    break, goto case N;]

[default:

    [Instructions)

    break, goto case N;]]

}
```

The expression of the switch statement contains the condition to be evaluated, which is used to decide which statement block is executed. The   statement   blocks   are   prefixed   with the case keyword, with a consistent expression defining the value to check for. If the constant expression in the case branch coincides with the expression of the switch statement, the statement or statements of the relevant case branch are executed. If this does not apply to any of the constant expressions, the default branch of the switch statement is executed, if available.

If there is no match between the expression of the switch statement and the constant expressions and the default branch is missing, the entire switch statement is ignored.

In a switch statement, if any instructions exist,
each case branch has an abort mechanism that
either sets the switch statement with the keyword

break;

leaves, or with

goto case N;

activates another case branch within the same switch statement.

Grinding

Loops are used in programming to execute instructions repeatedly. In jargon, repetitions are also called iterations. The functional counterpart to an iteration is recursion. In a recursion not statements and statement blocks are repeated, but complete functions or methods.

The Forefather Of The Loops - Goto Instruction

In the beginnings of computer science repetitions were realized by the goto statement. A goto statement, so to speak, jumps to a line and continues to execute the statements there. The structure was previously unstructured, the readability and clarity accordingly poor. Positions in the source code that can be jumped to are called jump labels. A jump label is a fixed name followed by a colon.

The syntax of a goto statement is:

goto jump label;

...

Label: instructions

As you noted above, I give the goto statement a negative image, and rightly so. Because it allows it to jump to any point in the program, which is not conducive to a structured structure with logical and comprehensible train of thought. This may not really matter in a one or two jump program, but as soon as you jump through a program, you quickly lose track.

You will now wonder why the programming language C# has kept the goto statement. This is because, in some situations, it is either imperative to solve a problem or at least greatly simplify the solution. Thus, with deeply nested loops, it may be necessary to leave them in certain program states - with one jump. But you should use the goto statement very sparingly and if possible resort to more elegant alternatives.

Continue Statement

The continue statement is the counterpart to the break statement. If you use the continue statement in a loop, it breaks off exactly at the position where the continue statement is located. This will continue with the next loop pass.

Chapter 7 - Methods, Parameters And Validity Of Variables

The larger and more complex a program becomes, the clearer it should be designed. The size and complexity of your programs will increase with your skills. So it is important to write the programs so that they are manageable and easy to maintain by breaking the structure of the programs into logical and physical modules. The advantage of this procedure is that these modules are implemented and optimized once in the program. For further use, you do not have to worry about how they work - the module becomes a *black box*.

Definition and Call

We already know that the programming language C# maps everything into classes. The functions, because they are elements of the classes, are called element functions. Over time, the term *method* for the element functions has prevailed. A method is thus a function within a class and belongs to the set of classes. However, many programmers do not distinguish exactly the designation rules in everyday language usage. We just have to remember that functions within a class are element functions or methods.

There are several ways to define methods.

Public - this type of method is used to communicate with the environment. They are visible to the outside and perform tasks that the environment demands.

Private - this type of method is used to execute repetitive statements and tasks within a class that cannot be called directly by the environment.

In this chapter we will deal exclusively with the second kind.

The method body contains the declarations and statements that are executed after the method is called.

Parameters Of A Method

Methods always fulfill a task and may require data. You can pass the data to a method using parameters that you want to process in the method. The way in which a method is supplied with data depends on the task. In principle, a distinction is made between value and reference parameters.

Defining Parameters

If a method is to work with parameters, these must be defined in the method header. Several parameters are separated by a comma. Each parameter requires its data type and parameter name.

```csharp
private static int add (int parameter1, int parameter2)

{

    Instructions;

}
```

If you call the method Add () as shown above, it requires two parameters of the type Integer. Note that the data types of the arguments are the same as those specified in the method definition.

From the point of view of the method, we always speak of parameters. Parameters are taken from the method definition.

In connection with the call of a method we speak of arguments. Arguments are passed to the method definition.

Types Of Parameters

The C# programming language essentially distinguishes two types of parameters. The first type are value parameters, as the example above shows. For a value parameter, only a copy of the value is passed. The called method can process the values, but has no direct influence on the parent function.

The second type are reference parameters. If a method is a reference parameter, it is defined by the reserved word ref.

Chapter 8 - Arrays

Data Management with Arrays

The programs you've seen so far have always had a relatively small, manageable amount of data. But what happens when you need to process more data in a program, such as a larger number of readings or hundreds of addresses that you read from a file or database? Do you need to define hundreds of individual variables?

int iMeasured1, iMeasured2, iMeasured3, iMeasured4...

No, of course there is a much more elegant solution to this problem: the arrays.

The efficient management of larger amounts of data in a program is an age-old problem that computer science has dealt with at an early stage. As a result of these efforts, we now know several basic models for storing data: lists, hashes, stacks, queues and even arrays. What sets the arrays apart from the other data structures is indexed access to the values stored in the array.

In C#, we can use the System.Array class to create arrays. For the sake of simplicity, we refer to variables that refer to array objects as arrays as well.

Sort Arrays

Arrays of numbers or strings can be conveniently sorted using the array.Sort () static array method. All you have to do is call the method and pass it the array instance you want to sort. The contained elements (numbers or strings) are then sorted in ascending order.

Search In Sorted Arrays

Arrays can manage larger amounts of data. Storing values or objects in an array, however, would be quite uninteresting if it were not possible to efficiently manipulate the elements in the array. These include:

The indexed access to individual elements,

Traversing the array elements in a loop and
finding a particular element in the array.

A simple but inefficient way to search for a name is to loop through the array and test for each element if it contains the name you are looking for. Such a search can be very fast (if the first element contains the name you are looking for), but it can take a long time (if the last element contains the name you are looking for or the name is not stored in the array).

A much more efficient search method is Binary Search, which assumes that the array is sorted. The binary search picks the middle element out of the array and checks if it is smaller or larger than the value you are looking for. Depending on the result of the comparison, searches are then continued for the same pattern in the lower or upper half of the array. In this way, the search space is halved at each step. The binary search is quite efficient; for an array with n elements, the search ends at the latest after $\log_2(n + 1)$ comparisons.

Fortunately, the System.Array class already has a ready-implemented static method of doing binary searches: BinarySearch (). When calling, you pass to the method the array to search and the value to find. As a result, you get back the index of the item containing the value you are looking for (or a value less than 0 if the value was not found).

Arrays As Parameters

Of course, arrays can also be passed as arguments to methods. The method defines a parameter of the corresponding array type:

static void values output (int [] param)

{

    foreach (int elem in param)

```
    WriteLine (elem);
```

}

When called, the array to be edited is simply passed to the parameter:

```
static void Main ()
```

{

```
    int [] anArray = {1, 2, 3, 4, 5,

                      6, 7, 8, 9, 10};

    Outputting values (anArray);
```

}

Composite Arrays

Arrays do not necessarily consist of a linear sequence of elements. Arrays can be multidimensional and they can contain other arrays as elements.

Multidimensional Arrays

One-dimensional arrays can be thought of as a linear sequence of values:

12345

Two-dimensional arrays can be thought of as values that resemble one another

Table arranged in rows and columns:

11 12 13 14 15

21 22 23 24 25

31 32 33 34 35

Three-dimensional arrays would be like cubes (with width, height, and depth), and with four-dimensional arrays, our imagination will be so slow.

To define a multidimensional array, specify the sizes of each dimension separated by commas in the square array brackets.

int [,] pay = new int [10,20];

For example, the above definition creates a two-dimensional array of 10 by 20 numbers. If you think of the array as a table, it would consist of 10 rows (first dimension) and 20 columns (second dimension).

Just as you define the array, you access its elements:
pay [5, 2] = 12;

Here, the third element in the sixth line is accessed (remember that the indexing of each dimension starts with 0).

There Is No Multidimensionality

In fact, there are no multidimensional arrays, because the working memory in which the elements of the array are created is, after all, only a linear, one-dimensional sequence of memory cells. So the multidimensionality of the arrays is something we just foolishly think about and that's why working with data like For example, the values of a table - which are inherently multi-dimensionally organized - are simplified.

Arrays Of Arrays

Multi-dimensional arrays have the special property that the elements of a dimension always have the same length. For example, a two-dimensional array consists of a certain number of rows, all of which have the same number of columns (second dimension).

In practice, however, one often has to do with data that is not quite as regularly arranged. For example, suppose that in the parquet of the previous section there are only 18 seats in the third and fourth rows.

Such a parquet can not be represented by a two-dimensional array, but rather as an array whose elements themselves are again arrays.

Chapter 9 - Fields

Fields are the data members of the class. They are defined by specifying an access specifier, the data type and the field name:

class CDemo

{

    int   field1; //   private   field
    internal double field2;...

Its scope is the class itself, which means that all methods of the class (including the constructor, destructor, properties) can access the fields.

When creating an instance, the generated object gets its own copy of each field in the class. The lifetime of a field is therefore equal to the lifetime of the object to which it belongs.

Initialization

The usual place to initialize fields is the constructor:

class CDemo

{

```
int field1;

internal CDemo ()

{

    field1 = 12;

}
```

...

However, from a technical point of view, this is not an initialization, but merely the assignment of an initial value. The field was already initialized when it was created (as it was created in the memory area of the object). The compiler assigns the fields their default values (for example 0 for int or double, false for bool). If you want a field to be initialized with a different value, you must specify it in the field definition:

```
class CDemo

{

    int field1 = 122;

    internal CDemo ()
```

```
{

    WriteLine (Field1); // returns 122

}
```

...

True initialization is faster than assigning an initial value in the constructor, but it is also less flexible because essentially only literals can be assigned.

Object Variables As Fields

Fields can also be of the type of a class. These fields are treated like all other fields. However, it is important to make sure that an object is assigned to the field before elements of that class are accessed through the field.

```
class CEclass

{

    int worth;

    ...

}
```

```csharp
class CDemo

{

    CEclass field;

    internal CDemo ()

    {

        field = new CEineClass (); // assignment of an object

        ...
```

Constant Fields

Constant fields are fields whose value can not be changed after the assignment of an initial value. In C# there are two ways to define a constant field:

const declaration

read-only declaration

The const declaration

class CDemo

```
{
    public const int field = 3;
```

In the definition, const fields must be initialized with a constant value, ie a literal or the value of another const field.

Thereafter, the value of the field can be queried, but not changed.

Chapter 10 - Heredity

Inheritance in the object-oriented sense means that a class passes on the elements defined in it to another class. Therefore, to see them as a mere means of convenient code reuse would be wrong and would not do it justice, because inheritance involves a number of other important object-oriented concepts, such as the overriding of methods, polymorphism, the abstract classes and the construction of class hierarchies. So we are dealing with a rather extensive network of interdependent and interdependent concepts based on inheritance. Nonetheless, inheritance itself is only a partial aspect of an even larger thematic complex - the question of which classes can relate to each other.

The next two days introduce you to the higher consecrations of object-oriented programming. Today begins with the basic syntax of inheritance and its implementation in simple programs. Tomorrow is dedicated to polymorphism, class hierarchies and interfaces.

Do not grieve if your head eventually becomes inaccessible given the variety of syntax forms and alternative techniques. With most of the techniques presented today and tomorrow, in practice, you will come into contact with them gradually, and it is quite natural (and so thought) that you will then go back to the relevant chapters and sub-chapters and these read again. But this should not be an excuse to skip the chapter now. Work through the chapters carefully and above all try to understand the concepts and ideas behind the techniques. Be sure to read the summaries at the end of the chapters, which will give you a concentrated overview of the concepts presented.

The Principle Of Inheritance

With inheritance, a new class is derived from an existing class.

The derived class inherits the elements of its base class.

Base class and derived class are normal classes. The terms "base class" and "derived class" refer only to what role the classes perform in inheritance:

The base class passes (inherits) its elements.

The derived class receives (inherits) the elements.

Looking at the inheritance from the perspective of the derived class, one also speaks of derivation.

The Basic Mechanism

Consider the following simple class:

class CBasis

{

```
public int value;

public void output ()

{

    Console.WriteLine ("value = {0}", value);

}

}
```

If you want to use this class as the base class of a new class, just append the name of the base class with a colon to the name of the new class when defining the new class.

```
class CAdirected: CBasis

{

    public void Increases ()

    {

        Value + = 10;

    }
```

}

Now, the derived class CAb, in addition to its self-defined method, Elevations (), also automatically has the elements of the base class. You Beach th that can be used as early as the methods of abge-initiated class inherited members even (in our example, the method increases increase () the field value that the class CAbgeleitet of the class CBasis inherited has).

The Meaning Of Inheritance

Throughout your career as a programmer, you will write a variety of classes to represent a wide range of objects and to solve a wide variety of tasks. At some point, you'll find that implementing a class that you want to create can very well use the functionality of a class you once wrote a long time ago. This raises the question of how the functionality representing a class can be meaningfully reused in the implementation of new classes. Object-oriented programming offers two different, complementary concepts in response to this question: inheritance and embedding.

While inheritance passes the elements of the existing class to the new class, embedding does nothing other than defining a field of the existing class type in the new class.

Even though you may not have been fully aware, you have been diligently using the concept of embedding, because whenever you declare a field of type class string in one of your classes, you have used the concept of embedding.

Some Important Facts

The issue of inheritance is quite complex, too complex to be summarized here in a few sentences. Therefore, this section is intended only to draw your attention to a few points and technical details that are quickly passed on when dealing with the far more important concepts, forgotten by the author, or taken for granted.

The base class inherits all elements defined in it except the constructors and destructors.

There is no way to influence the selection of inherited elements. (That is, you can not choose to inherit a particular constructor, nor can you exclude a field or method from inheritance.)

The base class is not changed by the inheritance. (The inherited elements are not missing later in the base class, nor do definitions in the derived class return to the base class.)

Inherited Elements Form Sub-Objects

When elements are passed by inheritance from a base class to a derived class, they form an independent subset, a base class part, in the derived class. On the one hand, the inheritance then makes the elements part of the derived class, on the other hand they remain base class elements once for all.

A small analogy should clarify this. Imagine being a car designer and builder. For people with the necessary change, you design and build fancy single models. For example, a wealthy Emir recently ordered the "Blue Eagle" model from you. As the basis for this model, you use the chassis and engine of a Jaguar E, chassis and interior make yourself. You sell the finished car for 120,000 euros to the Emir, who is now the proud owner of a "Blue Eagle". The "Blue Eagle" does not indicate that it was built on the basis of a Jaguar E. The components of the Jaguar have become parts of the »Blue Eagle«. However, there are still Jaguar elements, and if there is a problem with the chassis or engine, the Emir must contact a Jaguar dealer for repair.

Similarly, the inherited elements become part of the derived class, but without abandoning their descent from the base class. This has consequences for programming with inherited elements.

In principle, you can program with the inherited elements as well as with the elements that were defined directly in the derived class (see example: *inheritance.cs*). In certain situations, however, the basic class origin of the inherited elements comes to the fore and must be taken into account.

Why Do The Inherited Elements Form Sub-Objects?

The simple answer to this question is: inheritance is just an object-oriented concept and not a self-service store, in which one packs a field and a method into the shopping cart. After all, the author of the base class thought a bit about the definition of the class: He has written methods for controlled access to the fields and declared the fields as private, so that they can only be read or changed using the relevant methods. He also dumped subproblems in helper methods that are widely used by other methods in the class. Last but not least, he has written a constructor to correctly initialize the fields of the class.

Would inheritance work so that you could pick out individual elements of the basic classes or directly access inherited private elements for which the author of the base classes provided appropriate access methods in the methods of the derived class (see introductory example), breaking the complex structure of the base class and destroying the protections set up by the author of the base class, which should ensure the correct use of the base class elements. The actual, object-oriented mechanism of inheritance, on the other hand, ensures that this complex structure of effects, including the protective measures provided, is only inherited as a whole, as a subunit. Thus, the base class is protected from misuse and the author of the derived class from unnecessary errors in the use of the inherited elements.

Another reason for the object-oriented nature of inheritance is that on inheritance, other important object-oriented concepts, namely the construction of class hierarchies and polymorphism, build.

Three Access Levels

You now know that the inherited elements in the derived class retain their self-sufficiency and their access protection. Therefore, methods defined in the derived class can not access inherited private elements. What role the access specifiers still play in inheritance, this section will clarify. Particularly important for the understanding are the three central specifiers public, protected and private.

In the following discussion, we will exclude the access specifier internal as a (restricted) special case of public access. Public, protected and private

As a reminder, the purpose of the access specifiers is to protect individual elements from outside access, with the goal of making the use of the objects of the class safe and protecting the integrity of the objects.

Considering only the access specifiers public and private, the use and meaning of the specifiers are easy to grasp: there are only two levels of access, inside (ie within the class definition, which ultimately means "in the code of class methods") and outside (ie in code outside the class definition, which means that access is via an object of the class). The author of a class declares elements that are to be accessible from the outside as public, while marks elements that are to be used internally only by the methods of the class as private.

Three access levels

When you create an object from a derived class, the inherited elements in that object form a sub-object.

From the perspective of this sub-object, the three access levels are as follows: The sub-object itself is the inner world within which there is no access restriction (the sub-object's methods can access all other elements of the sub-object directly). The outside world consists of two layers. The first layer is the derived object. Out of this layer - that is, in the methods defined in the derived class - is allowed access to the public and protected, but not private, elements of the sub-object. The second layer is any outer code that creates an object of the derived class and uses it to access the elements of the sub-object. From this layer only the public elements can be accessed.

From the perspective of the derived object, there are also three levels. The first level is the object itself with the elements defined in its class. Within this level, direct, unrestricted access applies. The second level is the inherited base class subobject. Its elements can be directly accessed by the methods defined in the derived class, but with respect to the access specifiers. The third level is the outside world, which can access only an object variable and only the public elements of the object (own as well as inherited).

From the outside world's point of view, there is only a single object (the subobject is not perceived as such) and a form of access: via an object variable and only to public or internal elements (the public interface).

Access To Hidden Elements

Hidden elements - this applies not only to hiddenness in derived classes, but in general - continue to exist even after the occlusion, but can no longer be accessed because their name would be in the relevant area of validity (in the case of inheritance) this, for example, the derived class) has been connected to another element.

```
class CBasis

{

    protected double value;

}

class CAdirected: CBasis

{

    new public int value;

    public void value setting (int p)

    {
```

Value = p; // access to the newly defined element

```
    }

}
```

Here the element value obscures the inherited element of the same name. The valueSetting () method therefore accesses the value element defined in the CAb-routed class.

Inherited elements that were obscured in the derived class are still present and are still accessible. The programmer must precede the element name with only the keyword base, which represents the base class. This tells the compiler explicitly that it does not mean the element defined in the current class, but the same-named element that comes from the base class.

```
public void value setting (int p)

{

    base.value = p; // Access to the hidden base class
    member

}
```

The base keyword is mainly needed to invoke the base class version of the same name in hidden (or over-written) methods - as in the C number box method Insert () from the example above:

```
class CEigenerKK: CKummerkasten

{

new public void insert (string letter)

    {

            DateTime today = DateTime.Now;

            letter = today.ToString () + ":" +
            letter; base.Einwerfen (brief);

    }

}
```

The new warning

Whenever you obscure an inherited element in a derived class, the compiler generates a warning that alerts you of the occlusion and prompts you to either avoid it or tag it as intentional using the keyword new.

Perhaps one or the other reader will now think that this keyword is actually quite unnecessary, because after all, as a programmer, you should be able to ensure that you do not inadvertently cover up any inherited elements. Well, this may be true, as long as the programmer implements base classes and derived classes himself and the code remains quite clear. However, the more extensive the classes become, the more difficult it becomes, and it becomes nearly impossible for the programmer to derive from classes whose source code he does not know.

Consider the following scenario: You have acquired a library of classes to implement a inventory system. The library also includes a class CLieferauftrag, which does not quite meet your expectations. Since only the compiled library is available to you and you can not directly adapt the definition of the CLorder order class, you decide to assign your class a class CMasselivery order and provide the corresponding functionality (some additional fields and methods). add. In doing so, you overlook the fact that one of the methods you have added has the same signature as one of the methods inherited from CLieferauftrag. Without realizing it and without wanting it, you cover up the inherited method. Only the warning of the compiler makes you aware of it.

The warning also helps with naming conflicts due to changed base class versions. Let us stay with the example of the class CMeinLieferauftrag. These have been extended by an additional Discount () method compared to the base class CLorder order. Now the author of the Inventory Library delivers the newest version, in which the class CLjob order was also revised and supplemented with a discount () method. You install the new library version and recompile your code. The compiler detects that your discount () method obscures the now-existing discount () base class method and warns you.

So, if you receive a warning from the compiler to hide an inherited method, check whether the method really should be obscured. If so, set the keyword new before redefining the method and the compiler will no longer question the occlusion.

Inheritance vs. Embedding

The equivalent to inheritance is the embedding. Embedding means that a class defines fields that come from the data type of another class. While heredity is characterized by an "is-a" relationship, embedding corresponds to a "has-a" relationship.

For example, given three classes CMotor, CAuto and CSportwagen. What are the relationships between these classes?

There is a relationship between CAuto and CMotor, because a car has an engine. In the definition of the class CMotor this is expressed as follows:

class CMotor...

class CAuto

{

CMotor myMotor;

...

On the other hand, there is an "is a" relationship between the classes CAuto and CSportwagen. The class CSportwagen is derived from CAuto (and automatically inherits the CMotor element).

Nested Classes

From the fact that type definitions are allowed within classes, it follows that one class can be defined in another class. In addition to inheritance and embedding, this so-called nesting is the third form of the relationship between classes.

```
class CAussen

{

    public class Cin

    {

        ...

    }

    // other elements of CAussen

}
```

Chapter 11 – Projects

Making Code Decisions

Taking an example of banking application, we want to allow a withdrawal only if the amount to be withdrawn is less than or equal to the account balance, ie if the account balance is greater than or equal to the withdrawal amount, we must allow the transaction, otherwise we cannot allow the withdrawal. We need to do conditional execution of code.

In C #, we can execute conditional code using the if construct:

```
if (condition)
{
// This code will only execute if the condition is true
}
```

In our example, we want to execute the withdrawal logic only if the balance is greater than or equal to the withdrawal amount:

```
double balance = 100.0;
double valueBag = 10.0;
if (balance> = bag value)
{
// withdraw code.
}
```

The withdrawal code should decrease the account balance and display a message to the user indicating that the withdrawal was successful:

```
double balance = 100.0;
double valueBag = 10.0;
if (balance> = bag value)
```

```
{
balance = balance - valueSac;
MessageBox.Show ( "Withdrawal Successful" );
}
```

Note that if the account does not have sufficient balance to withdraw, the user is not warned. So we are in the following situation: "If the account has sufficient balance, I want to withdraw, otherwise I want to show the message Insufficient Balance to the user." To do this, we can use C # else :

```
if (balance> = bag value)
{
// withdraw code
}
else
{
MessageBox.Show ( "Insufficient Balance" );
}
```

More On Conditions

Notice the expression we pass to if : balance> = valueSak . In it we use the "greater or equal" operator. In addition, there are other comparison operators that we can use: greater (>), smaller (<), less or equal (<=), equal (==), and different (! =). We can also deny an if condition using the ! in front of the condition that will be denied.

In the previous chapter, we saw that a value has an associated type in C #: 10 is an int , "message" is a string . Similarly, the expression balance> = valueSak also has an associated type: the bool type , which can assume the values true or false . We can even store such a value in a variable:

bool canSacchar = (balance> = valueSac);

We can also perform some operations with bool values . We can, for example, verify that two conditions are true at the same time by using the && (AND) operator to make one and logical:

bool reallyCanSaccount = (balance> = valueSac) && (valueSac> 0);

When we need a logical OU, we use the || operator :

// this condition is true if (balance> = bag value) is true

// or if (bag value> 0) is true.

bool reallyCanSacc = = (balance> = valueSac) || (bag value> 0);

Thus we can build more complex conditions for an if . For example, we use the variable realmentePodeSacar declared in if that checks if the customer can withdraw or not:

```
if (reallyCanSac)
{
// withdraw code
}
else
{
MessageBox.Show ( "Insufficient Balance" );
}
```

Optional Exercises

1. What is the message and value of the balance variable after the following code has been executed?

```
double balance = 100.0;
double valueBag = 10.0;
if (balance> = bag value)
{
balance - = bag value;
```

```
MessageBox.Show ( "Withdrawal Successful" );
}
else
{
MessageBox.Show ( "Insufficient Balance" );
}
```
message: Withdrawal successful; balance: 90.0

message: Insufficient Balance; balance 90.0

message: Withdrawal successful; balance: 100.0

message: Insufficient Balance; balance 100.0

message: Withdrawal successful; balance: 10.0

2. What is the message and value of the balance variable after the following code has been executed?

```
double balance = 5.0;
double valueBag = 10.0;
if (balance> = bag value)
{
balance - = bag value;
MessageBox.Show ( "Withdrawal Successful" );
}
else
{
MessageBox.Show ( "Insufficient Balance" );
}
```

message: Withdrawal successful; balance: -5.0

message: Insufficient Balance; balance -5.0

message: Withdrawal successful; balance: 5.0

message: Insufficient Balance; balance 5.0

message: Withdrawal successful; balance: 10.0

3. In some cases we may have more than two possible decisions. The bank may, for example, decide that accounts with a balance of less than $ 1000 pay 1% of the maintenance fee, accounts with a balance of $ 1000 to $ 5000 pay 5%, and accounts with a balance of $ 5000 or more pay 10. %.

To represent this kind of situation, we can use C # else if , which works in conjunction with the if we already know. Here's what the situation described earlier would look like:

```
double rate;
if (balance <1000)
{
rate = 0.01;
}
else if (balance <= 5000)
{
rate = 0.05;
}
else
{
rate = 0.1;
}
```

C # will process the conditions in order until it finds one that is satisfied. That is, in the second condition of the code, we just need to check that balance is less than or equal to $ 5000, because if C # arrives in this condition is because it did not enter the first if , that is, we know that the balance is greater or equal to $ 1000 at this point.

Based on this, what will be the message displayed by the following code?

```
double balance = 500.0;
if (balance <0.0)
{
MessageBox.Show ( "You are in the negative!" );
}
else if (balance <1000000.0)
{
MessageBox.Show ( "You are a good customer" );
}
else
{
MessageBox.Show ( "You are a millionaire!" );
}
```

"You are in the negative!"

"You are a good customer"

No message

"You're a millionaire!"

"You're a good customer," followed by "You're a millionaire!"

4.   A person can only vote in Brazilian elections if he or she is over 16 years old and is a Brazilian citizen. Create a program with two variables, int age, Brazilian bool , and have the program tell you if the person is able to vote or not, according to the data in the variables.

5.   Create a program that has a doubleFiscalDateValue variable , and according to that value, the tax must be calculated. The calculation rules are:

If the value is less than or equal to 999, the tax must be 2%.

If the value is between 1000 and 2999, the tax should be 2.5%

If the value is between 3000 and 6999, the tax should be 2.8%

If it is greater than or equal to 7000, the tax must be 3%.

Print the tax on a MessageBox.

6. (Challenge) Given the following code:

```
int value = 15;
string message = "";
if (value> 10)
{
message = "Greater than ten";
}
else
{
message = "Less than ten;
}
MessageBox.Show (message);
```

There is a way to make this code if only one line, without using the word if and else. Research this and try it.

for ;

Repeating A Code Block

Back to the example from the previous class, suppose now that the same bank customer wants to know how much he will earn at the end of one year if he invests a value. The investment pays 1% of the amount invested per month.

For example, if the customer invests $ 1000 at the end of 12 months, it will be around $ 1126.82: in the first month, $ 1000 + $ 1000 1% = $ 1010, 00; in the second month, $ 1010 + $ 1010 1% = $ 1020.10; and so on. That is, to calculate how much he will have at the end of a year, we can multiply the amount invested 12 times by 1%.

To solve this problem, we need to make use of a control structure that repeats a given block of code until a condition is met. This structure is called loop.

To loop in C #, we will initially use the for statement. The for is an instruction that has three parts:

The first part is the initialization, in which we can declare and initialize a variable that will be used in the second part is the condition of the loop. As long as the loop condition is true, the loop will continue to execute;

The third part is the update, where we can update the variables that are used by for.

Each of the parts of the for is separated by one ; .

for (initialization; condition; update)
{
// This code will execute as long as the condition is true
}

Take the following code, for example, where we use a for that will repeat the calculation 12 times:

```
double valueInvested = 1000.0;
for ( int i = 1; i <= 12; i + = 1)
{
AmountInvested = AmountInvested * 1.01;
}
MessageBox.Show ( "Amount invested now is" + AmountInvested);
```

See that our for begins by initializing variable i with 1 and repeats the code inside it.

do ... while

as long as the value of i is less than or equal to 12, that is, it stops only when i is greater than 12. And note that with each iteration of this loop, the value of i increases (i + = 1) . In the end, the code inside the for will be repeated 12 times as we needed it.

The same program could be written using a while instead of a for :

```
double valueInvested = 1000.0;
int i = 1;
while (i <= 12)
{
AmountInvested = AmountInvested * 1.01;
i + = 1;
}
MessageBox.Show ( "Amount invested now is" + AmountInvested);
```

To Know More Of While

In C # when using while , the loop condition is checked before all loop turns, but what if we wanted to make sure the loop body is executed at least once? In this case, we can use another type of C # loop, while do :

```
of
{
// loop body
}
while (condition);
```

With do while the loop condition is only checked at the end of the loop, ie the loop body is

executed and then the condition is checked, then the body always is executed by the

least once.

To Know More Increment And Decrement

When we want to increment the value of an integer variable by one unit, we see that we have 2 options:

int value = 1;

value = value + 1;

// or value + = 1;

However, since incrementing the value of a variable is a common programming activity, C # gives us the ++ operator to do this work:

int value = 1;

++ value;

We also have the operator - which performs the decrement of a variable.

EXERCISES

1. What is the value displayed in the following code:

total int = 2;

for (int i = 0; i <5; i + = 1)

{

total = total * 2;

}

MessageBox.Show ("Total is:" + total);

2.   Make a C # program that prints the sum of the numbers from 1 to 1000.

3.   Make a C # program that prints all multiples of 3, between 1 and 100.

To find out if a number is a multiple of 3, you can do if (number% 3 == 0) .

4. (Optional) Write a C # program that sums all numbers from 1 to 100, skipping multiples of 3. The program should print the final result in a MessageBox.

What is the result?

5. (Optional) Write a C # program that prints all numbers that are divisible by 3 or 4 between 0 and 30.

6. (Optional) Make a C # program that prints the factorials 1 through 10. The factorial of a number n is n n-1 n-2 ... to n = 1.

The factorial of 0 is 1

The factorial of 1 is (0!) * 1 = 1

The factorial of 2 is (1!) * 2 = 2

The factorial of 3 is (2!) * 3 = 6

The factorial of 4 is (3!) * 4 = 24

Make a force that starts a variable n (number) as 1 and factorial (result) as 1 and ranges n from 1 to 10:

```
int factorial = 1;
for ( int n = 1; n <= 10; n ++)
{

}
```

7. (Optional) Make a C # program that prints the first numbers of the Fibonacci series to over 100. The Fibonacci series is as follows: 0, 1, 1, 2, 3, 5, 8, 13, 21 etc. To calculate it, the first element is worth 0, the second is worth 1, henceforth the nth element is worth the (n-1) -th element added to the (n-2) -th element (eg 8 = 5 + 3).

8. (Optional) Make a program that prints the following table using chained for s:

1

2 4

3 6 9

4 81216

nn * 2 n * 3 .... n * n

CLASSES AND OBJECTS

At this time, we want to represent several accounts in our bank. A bank account is usually composed of a number, name of the holder and balance. We can store this information in variables:

int AccountNumber1 = 1;

string holderDaAccount1 = "Joaquim José" ;

string holderAccount2 = "Silva Xavier" ;

double AccountAccount2 = 2500.0;

Note that because account information is spread across many different variables, it is very easy for us to mix this information into code. Also, imagine that before we add the account to the app we need to validate the holder's CPF. In this case we would need to call a function that performs this validation, but how can we ensure that this validation is always performed?

These points listed are some of the problems with procedural programming style. When working with procedural programming, application data is separated from business logic implementation, and it is very difficult to guarantee application data validations.

Organizing The Object Code

To start with object orientation, let's first think about what information describes a particular Account. Every bank account has a number, holder and balance. To represent the account with this information within the project, in C #, we need to create a class. Inside C # the class declaration is made using the word class followed by the class name we want to implement:

```
class Account
{
}
```

The code of the Account class , by convention, must be inside a file with the same name as the class, so the Account class will be placed in a file called Conta.cs .

Within this class we want to store the information that describes the accounts, we do that by declaring variables within the class, these variables are the attributes:

```
class Account
{
int number;
string holder;
double balance;
}
```

But in order for application code to read and write these attributes, we need to declare them using the word public :

```
Class Account
{
// number, holder and balance are attributes of the object public int number;
public string holder; public double balance;
}
```

In order to use the class we create within a windows form application, we need to create a new account in the form code, we do that using the new C # statement:

```
// form code
```

```csharp
private void button1_Click ( object sender, EventArgs e)
{
new Account ();
}
```

When we use new within the code of a class we are asking C # to create a new instance of Account in memory, that is, C # will allocate enough memory to store all Account information within the application's memory.

In addition, new has one more function, return reference, an arrow that points to the object in memory, which will be used to manipulate the Account created. We can store this reference within an Account variable :

```csharp
// form code
private void button1_Click ( object sender, EventArgs e)
{
Account c = new Account ();
}
```

to define the attribute values that will be stored in the Account , we need to access the object that lives in memory. We do this using the operator. C #, telling us which attribute we want to access. To, for example, save the value 1 as the account number we created, we use the following code:

```csharp
// form code

private void button1_Click ( object sender, EventArgs e)

{
```

```
Account c = new Account ();

c.number = 1;

}
```

With this code, we are navigating to the reference stored in variable c , and accessing the Number field of the Account object that lives in memory. Within this field we put the value 1. We can do the same for the other fields of the Account :

```
private void button1_Click ( object sender, EventArgs e)

{

Account c = new Account ();

c.number = 1;

holder = "victor" ;

c.saldo = 100;

}
```

Extracting Behavior Through Methods

Now that we have created the first application account, let's try some operations. The first operation we want to implement is the money-out operation. For this, as we saw in the previous chapter, we can use the C = - = operator :

Account c = new Account ();

c.number = 1;

holder = "victor" ;

c.saldo = 100;

// account ends with 50.0 balance c.saldo - = 50.0;

But what would happen if we tried to get 100.0 more out of this account?

c.saldo - = 100.0;

When we perform this second operation, the account will end with a balance of -50.0 , but in this system accounts cannot have a negative balance! Therefore, before we can withdraw money from the account, we need to check if it has sufficient balance.

if (c.saldo> = 100.0)

{

```
c.saldo - = 100.0;

}
```

Note that we will have to copy and paste this check at every point
of the application where we wish to make a withdrawal, but what
would happen if a withdrawal fee had to be charged? We would
have to modify all the points at which the code was copied. It
would be more interesting to isolate this code within an Account
behavior .

In addition to attributes, objects can also have methods. Methods
are blocks of code that isolate business logic from the object. Then
we can isolate the logic of the loot within a method
Saca of class Account .

To declare a method called Saca in the Account class , we use the
following syntax:

```
class Account

{

// declaration of attributes

public void Bag ()

{
```

```
// Method implementation

}

}
```

Within this method Saca , we will place the code of the serve logic.

```
public void Bag ()

{

if (c.saldo> = 100.0)

{

c.saldo - = 100.0;

}

}
```

However, in this code we have two problems: we cannot use variable c because it was declared in the form and not within the method and the value of the withdrawal is constant.

In this method Saca , we want to check the account balance on which the method was invoked. To access the reference in which a particular method was called, we use the word this . So to access the account balance, we can use this.saldo :

```
public void Bag ()

{

if ( this .saldo> = 100.0)

{

this .saldo - = 100.0;

}

}
```

We can use Saca inside the form with the following code:

```
Account c = new Account ();
```

// initialize account information c.saldo = 100.0;

// Now call the Saca method that was defined in class c.Saca ();

Now let's solve the problem of the fixed value of the withdrawal. When we want to pass a value to a method, we need to pass that value within the parentheses of the method call:

Account c = new Account ();

// initialize account information c.saldo = 100.0;

// Now call the Saca method that was defined in class c.Saca (10.0);

To receive the value that was passed in the Saca call , we need to declare an argument in the method. The argument is a variable declared within the parentheses of the method:

public void Bag (double value)

{

if (this .saldo> = value)

{

this .saldo - = value;

}

}

A method can have any number of arguments. We only need to separate the declaration of variables with a comma.

Returning Values Inside The Method

Now that we have put the Sack method into the Account class , we don't need to replicate the withdrawal validation code at all points of the code, we can simply use the method created, and if we need to modify the withdrawal logic, we can simply update the code. that method, a single point in the system.

But as implemented, the user of this method does not know whether or not the withdrawal was successful. We need to have the method return a Boolean value indicating whether or not the operation was successful. We will return true if the operation is successful and false otherwise.

When a method returns a value, the type of the returned value must be before the method name in its declaration. When a method returns no value, we use the void type .

```
// We are declaring that the method returns a value of type bool
public bool Sack ( double value)
{

// method implementation

}
```

Within the implementation of the method, we return a value using the word return followed by the value to be returned. So the implementation of Saca is as follows:

```
public bool Bag ( double value)

{

if ( this .saldo> = value)

{

this .saldo - = value;

return true ;

}

else

{

return false ;

}

}
```

When C # performs a return , it immediately returns the value and exits the method, so we can simplify the implementation of Saca to:

```csharp
public bool Bag ( double value)

{

if ( this .saldo> = value)

{

this .saldo - = value;

return true ;

}

return false ;

}
```

In the form we can retrieve the value returned by a method.

```csharp
Account c = new Account ();

// initialize the attributes
```

```
// If the account has sufficient balance, it will work with the value true

// otherwise, it will contain false

bool yielded Right = c.Saca (100.0);

if (it worked)

{

MessageBox.Show ( "Withdrawal Successful" );

}

else

{

MessageBox.Show ( "Insufficient Balance" );

}
```

Or we can use the method return directly within if :

```
Account c = new Account ();

// initialize the attributes
```

```
if (c.Saca (100.0))

{

MessageBox.Show ( "Withdrawal Successful" );

}

else

{

MessageBox.Show ( "Insufficient Balance" );

}
```

Standard Value Of Class Attributes

Now that we are done implementing the account withdrawal logic, let's also implement the deposit method. This method will not return any value and will be double argumented:

```
public void Deposits ( double value)

{

this .saldo + = value;
```

}

In the main application form, we can initialize the opening balance with the Deposits method :

Account c = new Account ();

c.Deposit (100.0);

In this code we are trying to deposit 100 reais into a newly created account and the Deposit method attempts to sum the 100.0 in the initial value of the account balance attribute. But what is the initial value of an attribute?

When we declare a variable in C #, it starts with an undefined value, so we can't use it until its value is initialized, but the language handles the attributes of a class differently. When we instantiate a class, all of its attributes are initialized to default values. Numeric values are initialized to zero, bool is initialized to false, and attributes that hold references are initialized to the empty reference (C # null value).

So in the example, when we deposit 100 reais into the newly created account, we are adding 100 to the initial account balance, which is zero, and then saving the result back to the account balance.

We can change the default value of a given attribute by placing an initial value in its declaration. To initialize the account with an initial balance of 100 reais instead of zero, we can use the following code:

```
class Account

{

public double balance = 100.0;

// other attributes and methods of the class

}
```

Now every account created will start with a starting balance of 100.0.

One Example: Download

Now let's try to implement the money transfer operation between two accounts. Within the Account class we will create one more method called Transfer , this method will receive the amount of the transfer and the accounts that will participate in the operation:

```
public void Transfers ( double amount, Source Account, Destination Account)

{
```

```
// implementation of the transfer

}
```

But do we really need to get both accounts as the method argument

Do you transfer ? Let's see how this method will be used within the form code:

```
Victor Account = new Account ();
```

```
// account initialization victor.saldo = 1000;
```

```
Account guilherme = new Account ();
```

```
// account initialization
```

```
// Now let's transfer the money from victor's account to
guilherme's victor.Transfer (10.0, victor, guilherme);
```

Note that using the method we are repeating the victor variable twice , but this is not necessary. We can use this to access the source account within the method, so in fact the Transfer method only needs to receive the destination account :

```
public void Transfer ( double amount, Destination Account)
```

```
{

// implementation of the transfer

}
```

Before we can withdraw money from the source account (this), we need to check if it has sufficient balance, just in this case we want to withdraw money from the source account and deposit it into the destiny:

```
public void Transfer ( double amount, Destination Account)

{

if ( this .saldo> = value)

{

this .saldo - = value;

destination.saldo + = value;

}

}
```

But this behavior of checking if the account has sufficient balance before making the withdrawal is the behavior of the Saca method that was previously implemented, plus adding a value to the balance is the Account Deposits operation . Therefore, we can use existing Saca and Deposit methods to implement Transfere :

public void Transfer (double amount, Destination Account)

{

if (this .Bag (value))

{

destination.Deposit (value);

}

}

Names Convention

When we create a class, it's important to remember that your code will be read by other developers on the team, so it is recommended that you follow naming standards.

When we create a class, the recommendation is to use Pascal Casing to name the class:

If the class name is composed of a single word, we capitalize the first letter (account becomes Account);

If the name consists of several words, all words joined by placing the first letter of each word capitalized (life insurance becomes SeguroDeVida).

In the case of method names, the convention is also to use Pascal Casing (for example, Draw and Deposit).

For method arguments, the recommendation is to use Pascal Casing but with the first letter in lowercase (Bag value , for example), a convention called Camel Casing.

You can find Microsoft recommendations at this link: http://msdn.microsoft.com/en-

us / library / ms229040 (v = vs.110) .aspx

Exercises

1. What does a class have?

Only the attributes of a system entity;

Only attributes or only methods of a system entity;

Only the methods of a system entity;

Attributes and methods of a system entity.

2. Let's create the Account class within the initial project using Visual Studio.

In Visual Studio, right-click the project name and select Add >

Class ...

Inside the window opened by Visual Studio, we need to define what is the name of the class we want to create. Choose Account Name :

After entering the class name, click the Add button . With this, Visual Studio will create a new file within the Project, Conta.cs . All code in the Account class will be inside this file:

class Account

{

// The class code is in here!

}

Now declare the following attributes within the Account : balance (double), holder (string), and

number (int).

3.   Which of the following commands instantiates a new Account? Account Account = Account ();

Account Account = new Account ();

Account Account = Account.new ();

4.   Considering the code:

Account c = new Account ();

c.saldo = 1000.0;

Which of the following lines adds 200 reais to this balance?

balance + = 200;

c.saldo + = 200;

Account c.saldo + = 200;

Balance Account + = 200;

5.   Now let's test the Account class we just created. Place a new button on the application form. Double-click this button to define which code will be executed at the button click.

private void button1_Click (object sender, EventArgs e)

{

// button action here.

}

Within the code of this button, instantiate a new Account and try some tests by filling in and showing its attributes through MessageBox.Show . For example:

private void button1_Click (object sender, EventArgs e)

{

AccountVictor Account = new Account ();

accountVictor.titular = "victor" ;

AccountVictor.number = 1;

accountVictor.saldo = 100.0;

MessageBox.Show (accountVictor.titular);

}

Try testing with multiple accounts and see that each account instance has its own attributes.

6.   Now let's implement methods in the Account class . We will start with the Deposit method , this method returns nothing and should receive a double argument that is the amount that will be deposited in the Account . Your class should look like this:

// inside Account.cs file

class Account

{

// declaration of attributes

public void Deposits (double value)

{

```
// what to put here in the implementation?



}



}
```

After implementing the Deposit method , implement the Saca
method as well . It also returns no value and receives a double
which is the amount that will be withdrawn from the account.

7.   Now let's test the methods we just created. In the button
action that we use to test the account, we will manipulate the
balance using the Deposit and Cashout methods :

```
private void button1_Click ( object sender, EventArgs e)

{

AccountVictor Account = new Account ();

accountVictor.titular = "victor" ;

AccountVictor.number = 1;

AccountVictor.Deposit (100);


MessageBox.Show ( "Balance:" + AccountVictor.saldo);
```

```
accountVictor.Saca (50.0);

MessageBox.Show ( "Balance:" + AccountVictor.saldo);

}
```

Try to make deposits and withdrawals in several different instances of Account , note that within the methods this variable has the reference value in which the method was invoked.

8. What is the following code output:

```
Mauricio account = new Account ();

mauricio.saldo = 2000.0;

Account guilherme = new Account ();

guilherme.saldo = 5000.0;

mauricio.saldo - = 200.0;

guilherme.saldo + = 200.0;

MessageBox.Show ( "mauricio =" + mauricio.saldo);

MessageBox.Show ( "guilherme =" + guilherme.saldo);

mauricio = 2200.0 and guilherme = 4800.0
```

mauricio = 2200.0 and guilherme = 5200.0

mauricio = 1800.0 and guilherme = 5000.0

mauricio = 1800.0 and guilherme = 5200.0

9. What is the following code output?

```
Mauricio account = new Account ();

mauricio.number = 1;

mauricio.titular = "Mauritius" ;

mauricio.saldo = 100.0;

Account mauricio2 = new Account ();

mauricio2.number = 1;

mauricio2.titular = "Mauritius" ;

mauricio2.saldo = 100.0;

if (mauricio == mauricio2)

{
```

```
MessageBox.Show ( "Accounts are the same" );

}

else

{

MessageBox.Show ( "Accounts are different" );

}
```

Bills are the same.

The accounts are different.

10. What is the following code output:

```
Mauricio account = new Account ();

mauricio.saldo = 2000.0;

Copy account = mauricio;

copy.saldo = 3000.0;

MessageBox.show ( "mauricio =" + mauricio.saldo);

MessageBox.show ( "copy =" + copy.saldo);
```

mauricio = 2000.0 and copy = 3000.0

mauricio = 3000.0 and copy = 2000.0

mauricio = 2000.0 and copy = 2000.0

mauricio = 3000.0 and copy = 3000.0

11.   (Optional) Implement the Transfer method that receives the transfer amount and the destination account. Have it reuse implementations of the Sack and Deposit methods .

12.   (Optional) Let's add validation to   the Account Drawout method . Modify the Draw method so that it does not withdraw if the current account balance is less than the amount

received as an argument.

13.   (Optional) Modify the Validate Draw method to return true if the draw was successful and false otherwise. Then modify the account test button code to use the value returned by the Sack method to display a message to the user. If the withdrawal is successful, we want to show the message "Withdrawal successful", otherwise we will show "Insufficient Balance"

14.   (Optional) Now change the Sack method of the Account class. Limit the withdrawal amount to $ 200 if the client is underage.

Remember that you still need to validate if the amount to be withdrawn is less than or equal to the customer's current balance and is greater than $ 0.00.

Class Composition

When we open a bank account, we have to provide a lot of information: name, social security number, ID and address.

We have seen that when we want to store information in a class, we must create attributes. But in which class put these new attributes? Clearly this information does not belong to an Account . This data belongs to the account holder, ie this information belongs to the bank customer .

Then we must store them in a Customer class .

class Customer

{

public string name;

public string cpf;

```
public string rg;

public string address;

}
```

We also know that every account is associated with a customer, that is, the account holds a reference to the associated customer.

```
class Account

{

// other attributes of the public Account Holder Customer;

// account behaviors

}
```

Now, when we create an account, we can also place its holder.

```
Customer victor = new Customer ();

victor.name = "victor" ;

Account oneAccount = new Account ();
```

a AccountAccount = victor;

We also saw that the holder attribute holds a reference (arrow) to a Client instance (object in memory). Therefore, assigning an AccountAccount = victor is copying the reference from the victor variable to the holder attribute .

We may modify Customer's attributes by reference stored in the holder attribute.

the Account .

Customer victor = new Customer ();

victor.name = "victor" ;

Account oneAccount = new Account ();

a AccountAccount = victor;

aHeadAccount.rg = "12345678-9" ;

// Display the name victor MessageBox.Show (a.Account.name);

// Display the text 12345678-9 MessageBox.Show (victor.rg);

6.9 EXERCISES

1.   Create the Client class containing the attributes name (string), rg (string), cpf (string) and address (string). Modify the Account class and make its holder attribute of type

Client instead of string .

Be careful. After this modification we will not be able to assign the customer name directly to the Account holder attribute . To define the name of the holder, we will need a code similar to the following:

Account Account = new Account ();

Client Client = new Client ();

holder.account = customer;

account.titular.name = "Victor" ;

2. What output will be printed when executing the following code snippet?

Account oneAccount = new Account ();

Customer guilherme = new Customer ();

guilherme.name = "Guilherme Silveira" ;

oneAccount.table = guilherme;

MessageBox.Show (an account.holder.name);

Guilherme Silveira

A message box will appear without any message.

The code does not compile

3. What output will be printed when executing the following code snippet?

Account oneAccount = new Account ();

Customer guilherme = new Customer ();

guilherme.rg = "12345678-9" ;

oneAccount.table = guilherme;

aHeadAccount.rg = "98765432-1" ;

MessageBox.Show (guilherme.rg);

98765432-1
12345678-9

rg

Nothing will print

4.   (Optional) Create one more attribute in the Customer class that keeps the person's age. In our case, age is an integer.

Also create a behavior (method) with the name EhMajorDeath in the Client class that takes no arguments and returns a boolean indicating whether the client is of legal age or not. When is a person of legal age in Brazil?

ENCAPSULATION AND ACCESS MODIFIERS

At this time, our Account class has a number , balance, and a holding customer , and behaviors that allow you to withdraw and deposit:

class Account

{

public int number;

public double balance;

```
public Owner;

public void Bag ( double value) {

this .saldo - = value;

}

public void Deposits ( double value) {

this .saldo + = value;

}

}
```

If we wish to withdraw or deposit to any Account , we will:

```
account.Saca (100.0);

deposit account (250.0);
```

But what happens if a team member does:

```
account.saldo = 100.0;
```

Nothing prevents us from accessing the attributes directly. In three distinct parts of our software we have such code:

// in a file account.saldo - = 100.0;

// in another file account.saldo - = 250.0;

// in another file account.saldo - = 371.0;

Now imagine that the bank changes the withdrawal rule: now with each withdrawal the bank will charge 0.10 cents. That is, if the user withdraws 10.0 reais, it is necessary to withdraw from his account 10.10 reais. We have to change all points of our application that access this attribute! But our code base can

It is very large and it is very common to forget where and who is accessing this attribute, leaving bugs every time we forget to change somewhere. If we have this line spread 300 times in our system, we need to find all 300 lines and make the change. Very complicated and costly!

What would happen when we use the Saca () method :

// in an account file. Bag (100.0);

// in another file account.Saca (250.0);

// in another file account.Saca (371.0);

How would we reflect the change in the 10-cent withdrawal rule? We only need to change the Saca () method once , instead of changing all lines that access the attribute directly!

Encapsulation

By releasing access to the attributes of the Account class , we are allowing any programmer to make their own unsafe implementation of the loot logic any way they want. If the modification of the attribute was restricted to the class that declares it, everyone who wanted to withdraw or deposit money in the account would have to do so by class methods. In this case, if the withdrawal rule changes in the future, we will only modify the Sack method.

In object orientation, hiding the implementation details of a class is a concept known as encapsulation. Because the implementation details of the class are hidden, all access must be done through its public methods. We don't let others know HOW the class does her job, showing only WHAT she does.

See the line Conta.Saca (100.0); . We know what this method does for its name. But how he does his job will only know if we get into his implementation. Therefore, the behavior is encapsulated in this method.

But we haven't solved the problem of preventing programmers from directly using the attribute yet. Anyone can still execute the code below:

account.saldo - = 371.0;

For this we need to hide the attribute. We want to keep it private so that only the Account class itself can use it. In this case we want to modify access to the attribute so that it is private, private:

class Account

{

// other attributes here

.

private double balance;

public void Bag (double value) {

this .saldo - = value;

}

public void Deposits (double value) {

this .saldo + = value;

}

}

Private attributes and methods are accessed only by the class itself. That is, the Saca () method , for example, can make changes to it. But other classes can't access it directly! The compiler does not allow it!

The attributes of a class are implementation details, so we will mark all account attributes with the word private:

class Account

{

private int number;

private double balance;

private Customer holder;

public void Bag (double value) {

this .saldo - = value;

}

public void Deposits (double value) {

```
this .saldo + = value;
```

```
}
```

```
}
```

Great. Now the programmer is forced to go through the methods to manipulate the balance . If we try, for example, to type in the Account balance from a form code, we will have a compilation error:

```
Account c = new Account ();
```

```
// The line below generates a compilation error c.saldo = 100.0;
```

But now we have another problem. If we want to display the balance we will not be able to. The private blocks both the writing, the reading!
Controlling Access To Properties

We saw that we can prohibit external access to an attribute using C # private, but private also blocks the reading of the attribute, so to retrieve its value, we need a new method within the class that will return the current value of the attribute:

```
class Account
```

```
{
```

```
private double balance;

private int number;

// other account attributes and methods

public double PegaSaldo ()

{

return this .saldo;

}

}
```

Now to show the balance to the user, we would use the following code:

```
Account Account = new Account ();

// initialize the account

MessageBox.Show ( "balance:" + account. HandleSaldo ());
```

Also, the account needs a number, but as it has been declared private , we cannot access it directly. We'll need a new method to do this work:

```
class Account

{

private int number;

// other attributes and methods of the account public void
PutsNumber ( int number)

{

this .number = number;

}

}
```

To put the number on the account, we would have to execute this code:

```
Account Account = new Account ();

account.Place Number (1100);

// use account in code
```

Note that this allows us to control all access to the Account class, but to write or read the value of an attribute we need to use the methods. Ideally we should use a syntax similar to that of attribute access, but with the control that the method gives us. To solve this problem, C # gives us the properties.

The declaration of a property is similar to the declaration of a attribute, but we need to talk about what should be done in reading (get) and writing (September) property

```csharp
class Account

{

private int number;

public int Number

{

get

{

// code to read property

}

set

{
```

```
// code to write in property


}


}


}
```

In reading the property, we want to return the value of the Account number attribute :

```
class Account


{


private int number;


public int Number


{


get


{


return this .number;


}
```

```
}
```

```
}
```

With this, we can read the Number property with the following code:

```
Account c = new Account ();
```

```
MessageBox.Show ( "number:" + c.Number);
```

Note that access was equal to attribute access, but when we try to read the value of a property we are actually executing a code block (get property) of the Account class . To set the account number, we will use the code:

```
Account c = new Account ();
```

```
c.Number = 1;
```

When we try to write to a property, C # uses the set block to store its value. Within the set block , the value that has been assigned to the property is within a variable called value , so we can implement the set as follows:

```
class Account
```

```
{

private int number;

public int Number

{

// get statement

set

{

this .number = value ;

}

}

}
```

We can also declare a property that has only get , without set . In this case, we are declaring a property that can be read but not writable. With properties we can completely control access to class attributes using the attribute access syntax.

Simplifying Property Statement With Self-Implemented Properties

Using properties, we can control access to class information, but as we have seen, declaring a property is quite laborious. We need an attribute to store its value, and we need to declare get and set .

To make it easier to declare properties, starting with C # 3.0, we have properties that are automatically implemented by the compiler, the auto-implemented properties. To declare an auto-implemented property to expose the account number, we use the following code:

```
class Account

{

public int Number { get ; set ; }

}
```

This code causes the compiler to declare an attribute of type int (whose name is known only to the compiler) and generate the code for the Number property with a get and a set that read and write to the declared attribute. Note that by using auto-implemented properties, we can only access the value of the declared attribute through the property.

Every time we declare an auto-implemented property, we always need to declare a get and a set for the property, but we can control the visibility of both get and set .

For example, in the case of balance, we want to allow anyone to read the account balance, but only the account itself can change it. In this case, we use the following code:

```
class Account

{

// other properties

// get is public and can be accessed by any class

// set is private and therefore can only be used by the account.
public double Balance { get ; private set ; }

// rest of class code.

}
```

Now let's look at code that tries to read and write in the properties we declare:

```
Account c = new Account ();

c.Number = 1; // it works because the number set is public
```

MessageBox.Show ("number:" + c.Number); // works because Number get is public

c.Saldo = 100.0; // Balance set is private, so we have an error
MessageBox.Show ("balance" + c.Saldo); // works because Balance get is public.

Note that both by declaring properties explicitly and using auto-implemented properties, we have complete control over what information will be exposed by the class.

So we should use properties every time we want to expose some class information. We should never expose class attributes (using public) because we never want to expose the implementation details of the class.

Name Convention For Property

The naming convention defined for C # properties is the same naming convention used for classes, ie using Pascal Casing (all words in the name are concatenated and each word has an initial capital letter, for example: bank number => BankNumber)

Exercises

1. What is the behavior of the attribute below:

public int Number { get ; private set ; }

The number can be read, but cannot be changed by other classes.

The number cannot be read, but can be changed by other classes.

The number can neither be read nor changed by other classes.

The number can be read and changed by other classes.

2. About the code below it is valid to state that ...

Account c = new Account ();

double valueDispose = 200.0;

c.Salde + = valueDispose;

The deposit operation has been implemented correctly.

The deposit operation is not encapsulated and may cause future maintenance problems.

The deposit operation is not encapsulated, making future code maintenance easier.

3.   What is encapsulation?

It's very clear to everyone how the class does its job.

It is the use of Properties in any of its variations.

It is manipulating and changing attributes directly, without going through a specific method.

It is hiding HOW the class / method does its task. If the rule changes, we have to change only one point of the code.

4. What is the problem with the attribute below:

public double Balance { get ; set ; }

None. It is encapsulated, after all we use Properties.

Instead of public , we should use private .

The Balance attribute can be manipulated by other classes. This goes against the encapsulation rule. It's no use creating Properties and allowing all attributes to be modified by the other classes.

5.   Turn the attributes of the Account class into properties. Allow the account balance to be read but not change outside the class, also change the code of the classes that use the account to access properties instead of attributes directly.

Conclusion

Thank you for making it through to the end of *C#*, let's hope it was informative and able to provide you with all of the tools you need to achieve your goals whatever they may be.

All C# classes, be they part of the.NET Framework or redefined by you, go back to a common base class: System.Object.

Classes defined without a base class are automatically assigned System.Object as a direct base class; derived classes inherit System.Object over the last of their base classes.

But if all C# classes are directly or indirectly derived from System.Object, it means that they all inherited the methods and fields of System.Object. Reason enough to take a look at the public and protected elements of System.Object.

The derived class inherits all elements of its base class, with the exception of the constructors and the destructor. It can directly access the inherited public, internal, protected, and internal protected elements, not the private elements.

The derived class can obscure or overload inherited items. Covered elements continue to exist in the derived class and can be called using the keyword base.

In C#, all classes automatically inherit the elements of the System.Object class. This provides a basic functionality common to all C# objects (support for copying, comparing and converting to strings).

Classes can implement any number of interfaces as long as they provide the methods inherited from the interfaces with appropriate statement parts.

Finally, if you found this book useful in any way, a review on Amazon is always appreciated!

Made in the USA
Columbia, SC
01 July 2020